D1345250

Astrology

Hugh Arthur

TREASURE PRESS

To Monica

ACKNOWLEDGEMENTS

Benrido Company, Kyoto 15; Biblioteca Apostolica Vaticana, Rome 11; Bibliothèque Nationale, Paris 21; British Museum, London 13; W. Foulsham & Co. Ltd 80–81; Photographie Giraudon, Paris 19, 117; David A. Hardy, Birmingham 121; Mansell Collection, London 17; National Portrait Gallery, London 102; Orlandini, Modena 35, 37, 39, 41, 43, 45, 47; Pictorial Press, London 29; Ann Ronan Picture Library, Loughton – E. P. Gold–Schmidt & Co. Ltd 113; Tony Stone Associates, London 9; Z.E.F.A., London 103.

First published in Great Britain 1982 by
Hamlyn Paperbacks

This edition first published in Great Britain 1989 by
Treasure Press
Michelin House
81 Fulham Road
London SW3 6RB

ISBN 1 85051 439 9

Printed in Hong Kong

Contents

THE HISTORY OF ASTROLOGY

Origins in Mesopotamia

When in about 2100 BC Abraham, the traditional founder of the Hebrew race, left Ur of the Chaldees, astrology may already have been a thousand years old. The patriarch was originally almost certainly a moon-worshipper, for the Israelites, his descendants, celebrated the new moon every month. The seventh day, later rationalized into the day of rest of the creator of the universe after his work was finished, is thought to have at first marked each quarter of the moon as it waxed and waned in its twenty-eight or four groups of seven days.

The migration of Abraham to Harran, north-east of Ur, was caused, some scholars think, by a religious revolution in Ur which replaced the worship of the moon-god Sîn by a cult of the sun.

Whatever the reason, it was in the Fertile Crescent, where the Euphrates and Tigris watered the lands of Mesopotamia and the Jordan the length of Palestine, and in Egypt, where the Nile brought forth its abundant harvests, that civilizations were cradled and grew. Nearly as old as these civilizations and as soon as men learned to sow seeds rather than live as nomads, there came into being the study of the heavenly bodies which governed the seasons upon which the crops depended. Thus the royal art of astronomy–astrology was born, the first exact science to be studied in the history of mankind.

It was royal because in Ur, a city of Sumer, that part of Mesopotamia immediately north of the Persian Gulf, astrology was used to divine the omens of king and nation, but for no other purpose. North of Sumer was Babylonia, and in these two countries, some of whose cities are thought to have existed as early as 5000 BC, were laid the foundations of the astrology from which the modern art has descended. The sun and moon were early venerated, the one for its obvious effects on the growth of crops, the other for its repeated and exact pattern by which time could be measured. The backcloth of heaven, with its fixed constellations, seemed unchanging. But in the wonderfully clear skies of Mesopotamia the movement of stars which were not fixed but seemed to traverse regular paths in the firmament was soon observed and the planets Mercury, Venus,

Mars, Jupiter, and Saturn came to be known. The zone in which these paths lay, the belt of the zodiac, is said by some to have been known for thousands of years, although most modern authorities ascribe its recognition to Greek science of the fifth and sixth centuries BC.

Venus, shining both as the morning and evening star, was identified by the Sumerians with Innin or Inanna, the Lady of Heaven, and by the Babylonians with Ishtar, goddess of war and carnage, in her morning appearance, but of love, procreation, fertility, gentleness, and luxury in the evening. She was the daughter of Ṣîn, the moon-god, and sister of the sun-god, Utu or Shamash. The red planet of Mars was the Babylonian Nergal, also associated with war, pestilence and destruction, and ruler of the underworld. The twinkling star, Mercury, was the Babylonian Nabu. Jupiter was Marduk, Saturn Ninib, and there was also a sky god called Anum.

There may have been some confusion of thought as to whether the planets were gods themselves or their palaces in

The Fertile Crescent

space. The planets were carefully observed from temples raised high on towers or ziggurats, so mighty even in their ruins today that it is easy to see how they suggested the legend of a tower of Babel whose top should reach heaven. From their summits the 'writing of heaven' was observed with such skill that the record of eclipses is said to have gone back to 747 BC, and by early in the first millennium BC the knowledge of the sun's annual course, the phases of the moon, and the periodicity of certain planets were known. By the fifth century some knowledge of the zodiacal belt had been acquired. Reports of earthly phenomena apparently resulting from movements of the gods in the heavens were recorded in writings known as the *Enuma Anu Ellil.* Prediction quickly followed, at first of events of a general nature such as wars and floods. Later they became more precise: the birth horoscopes of individual kings were cast, some of which exist in cuneiform writings to this day.

Mesopotamian astrology survived in part until the twelfth or thirteenth century AD, when it was destroyed by the Mongol invasions. In the Koran the religious community known as Sabians, descendants of the moon-worshippers of Abraham's time, is mentioned as one of the sects permitted to exist by Islam. The Sabians were tolerated because they recognized the existence of a supreme deity who had, however, no contact with mankind, but, after creating the universe, had placed it under the rule of the planets, each of which had special influence over a particular type of character.

From Mesopotamia astrology spread eastwards to India about the sixth century BC and reached China soon afterwards (although there may have been some influence centuries before), penetrated to Indo-China and even, some claim, affected early civilization in the Americas. Moving westwards, it took root in Egypt and Greece. Meanwhile, independently of Babylon and Sumer, primitive peoples in western Europe had marked the solstices and other astronomical events by systems of megaliths, some of which date back to 2000 BC. Later, in Mexico, the Mayas had from about AD 300 developed an even more accurate knowledge of astronomy than the Babylonians, with a calendar of 365 days and a zodiac of thirteen signs.

(Opposite) Reconstruction of a ziggurat

The influence of Greece

Since Greek culture, through the conquests of Alexander the Great (356–323 BC), affected the Near and Middle East, India, Egypt and, later, western European civilization, its influence can scarcely be overestimated. The appearance and characteristics of the planets inspired the Greeks in much the same way as they had Babylonians, and many of the deities allocated to the heavenly bodies were as close as they could be to Babylonian ideas. Ishtar, the morning and evening star, became Aphrodite and, when Rome accepted astrology, Venus, goddess of love and desire. Nabu was transformed into Greek Hermes and Roman Mercury, the messenger of the gods, whose winged feet twinkled like his planet as he sped about his work. Nergal became Mars, both deities of war and destruction, lords of the blood-red planet. Marduk, chief of the Babylonian deities, appropriately changed to Greek Zeus and Roman Jupiter, 'father of gods and men,' patrons of the luminous star. Babylonian Ninib, Greek Kronos and Roman Saturn ruled the brilliant star, the Indicator.

To the astral gods of the Babylonians the Greeks added catasterism, the identification of other stars with the heroes, heroines, and demigods of mythology. The two civilizations pollinated each other in the realm of astrological ideas. Alexander the Great, mourning at the age of thirty-two that there were no more worlds for him to conquer, forgot the kingdoms of the mind. After his death, not only was there a diffusion of Greek ideas east, south, and west, but the Greeks themselves were opened to influences from lands which, but for Alexander, might have remained intellectually isolated for centuries.

In 280 BC, about forty years after his death, a Chaldean priest named Berosus brought astrology to Greece, and Greece stamped the art with the die of its own genius. At Alexandria the Greek astronomer Ptolemy composed the *Almagest* and *Tetrabiblos*, the first definitive astrological treatises still in existence.

The *Tetrabiblos* ('Four Books') informs the reader that the earth is surrounded by the ambient, or power derived from aetherial nature. By and through this, forces are transmitted from the heavenly bodies. These affect procreation, fertility, and the processes of growth, moulding the forms of all developing creatures by such of them as are present at the time. Calculations of the future positions of the stars and planets can thus make prediction possible, enabling the knowledgeable physician to cure illness and rendering all the skill of the ignorant of no avail. Ptolemy lists the favourable stars ('benefics') and the unfavourable ('malefics') – stars may be either according to their positions and the relative positions of others – and gives the different characteristics of the signs of the zodiac and of the houses, the significance of which is recounted in Chapter Two.

Book II of the *Tetrabiblos* applies the theory of Book I to nations and cities, very much in the fashion of the old Babylonian astrology. Books III and IV deal with individuals, and it was with these that the Greeks brought astrology to the common man. No longer was it the privilege of kings to have the future foretold for them. Now it became the right of every man who could afford the fee of a 'Chaldean' (astrologer). His

Stonehenge: a megalithic observatory

horoscope would determine his temperament, indicate the possible form of his death – for Saturn produced consumption and rheumatism, Jupiter apoplexy and heart disease, and Mars strokes – and even estimate his life span.

However, Egypt had possessed its own astronomy before Ptolemy. From possibly as early as 2000 BC it had developed a calendar of twelve months of thirty days, each with five days added at the end of the year, a system subsequently adopted by the Greeks. Each day and night were divided into twelve equal parts, the length of which varied according to the time of year.

Astrology was brought to Egypt by the Persians in the sixth century BC, and during the Hellenistic period, 330 to 30 BC, the Egyptians accepted the view that the stars ruled human destiny. Mesopotamian influence probably helped in this, and Egypt developed a form of astral religion, with features of its own, which affected Greece and, later, Rome. Thirty-six stars called decans were selected. Rising at ten-day intervals, each was governed by a spirit who ruled the ten-day period. Later these became ten-degree subdivisions of the twelve thirty-degree zodiacal signs, which Egypt had received in the third century BC, helping to support the idea that every moment of time had its individual quality. Fifty-nine deities in all presided over various units of time.

About 150 BC an astrological treatise by a fictitious priest and king, called respectively Petosiris and Nechepso, ascribed each day of the week to a planet. Even more important than this was the collection of texts made between 50 BC and AD 150 and attributed to Hermes, the Greek equivalent of the Egyptian god Thoth. The concern of the ordinary man with astrology is shown by the fact that horoscopes were sometimes inscribed on tombs.

Astrology in the East

In the East Babylonian astrology influenced the *Vedas*, the sacred scriptures of Hinduism written by 1000 BC and allegedly composed by the seven Rishis or Shining Ones, the stars of the Great Bear. With the spread of Greek influence in India

(Opposite) Illustration from Ptolemy's *Tetrabiblos*, Byzantine, AD 820

following Alexander's conquests, individual horoscopes came into fashion, but it was not until six centuries later that Indian astrology, still influenced by Greek, was able to evolve fully. But it had its own genius, developing the Nakshatras, the lunar mansions, more completely than any other country. The ecliptic was divided into twenty-eight, one division for each day of the lunar month and each with its own significance, as important for prognostication as the signs of the zodiac. India had its Ptolemy in Vahara Mihara who, in the sixth century AD, summarized all the astronomical knowledge and astrological theory of the time, showing the marked influence of the Greeks on the nature of the Indian gods, the names of the days of the week, the characteristics of the zodiacal signs, and the system of houses relating to the business of daily living.

Hinduism added to astrology the idea of *karma* (the inevitable results that a man's actions bring upon himself during the whole of his existence) and reincarnation, which develops his *karma* through a multiplicity of lives. Thus the results of actions in previous incarnations and of deeds in the present life affected by past lives, together with future actions of this life and of others yet to be, could be indicated by the stars. These could reveal the stage in his spiritual development that an individual had attained.

The Chinese adopted the idea of forecasting events by the stars but developed their astronomy independently of this. They brought to astrology the two principles of positive yang (masculinity, light, and motion) and negative yin (femininity, darkness, and repose), which play so large a part in Chinese thought generally. They divided the sky into five 'palaces,' a central region round the pole and four equatorial divisions, which corresponded to the four seasons. Twelve signs, named Tiger, Hare, Dragon, Serpent, Horse, Sheep, Monkey, Hen, Dog, Pig, Rat, and Ox, alternately having the qualities of yang and yin, were based on divisions of the equator, not of the sky, as with the zodiac. Each of these gave its name to a double-hour in daily time and also to a month. They combined with ten planetary signs, five under yang and five under yin, to give sixty double signs by permutations of the yang planet and equatorial signs in one division and the yin signs in another. There were twenty-eight lunar 'mansions', reminiscent of the

Aries (the Ram) taken from a Sanskrit manuscript

Indian system in that each represented one day of the lunar month. They were grouped under the twelve animal signs – so many mansions to each sign.

The Chinese also had an intricate system of correspondences, the planet Jupiter, for example, being associated with the element wood, the colour green, and the stars. Further complications were introduced by the application of the yang principle to each element in its man-modified state (wooden furniture and houses, for example) and the yin in its natural condition (growing trees). Individual horoscopes appeared late in China – about the first century AD.

The Roman experience

Meanwhile, in the West, the Greeks were developing the detailed, complex, and apparently scientific system, combining Babylonian, Egyptian, and their own principles, which is the ancestor of European astrology. Not only science gave its accolade to the system. It also received the support of philosophy, religion and medicine. The Stoic doctrine of universal 'sympathy' between the microcosm (man) and the macrocosm (the universe) seemed both to support and be supported by astrology. Mithraism, an ancient Persian religion, introduced to the West in the first century BC, and later one of Christianity's most dangerous rivals, initiated its worshippers into successive stages representing the soul's journey through the seven planetary realms. In its rites the celebrants wore masks portraying the animals of the zodiac. Melothesia, the science which places each portion of the body under the domination of the stars and the zodiac, became part of standard medical practice.

In spite of its acceptance of Greek culture, Rome did not take to astrology, which came to it in the second century BC, without some resistance. The official augurs, who divined by different methods such as the flight of birds or the entrails of animals, at first opposed the new science, and officialdom, fearing their influence upon the populace, frequently banished astrologers. But it gained favour among the people who welcomed 'Chaldeans' who could tell their fortunes by the stars, and was made respectable by the great scholar-astrologer, Publius Nigiolius Figulus (99–45 BC), a friend of Cicero and, as a Pythagorean philosopher, a fatalist. He wrote two books on the Eastern and Greek astrological systems. Another writer was Manilius (a pseudonym) who wrote verses called *Astronomics* during the reign of Augustus, describing the universe as the

A mandala in the Horyuji Temple, Japan

work of an all-powerful creator who gave signs by which nations could learn their destinies and men their characters. He also dealt with astrological anatomy, the basis of astro-medicine.

The Roman emperors regarded astrology with suspicion, since it could reveal the fate of leaders to enemies plotting their downfall. Tiberius used it as an offensive weapon, casting the horoscopes of possible rivals, and Domitian executed one such and also an astrologer whose forecast for him was unfavour-able. Septimius Severus married a Syrian lady whom astro-logers foretold would be the wife of a king and became emperor. Popular belief in astrology was given religious sanction by Gnosticism in various forms, which had in common the idea of the soul's escaping from this wicked world of materialism through the spheres to perfect spirituality beyond. Philosophy again added its weight to the cause in the person of Plotinus, founder of Neo-Platonism, who settled in Rome in AD 244. He believed that the stars were living beings who had an influence on human lives, but was unwilling to surrender the idea of free will. He reconciled the contradiction by a concept which had much of the quality of the modern theory of synchronicity – the celestial movements were signs, not causes, of the future.

Astrology and religious belief

Judaism had little time for astrology. The jealous worshippers of Jehovah continually strove to rid the Chosen People of rival spirit mediums, soothsayers, magicians, and diviners. Yet there are many references to astral influence in the Old Testament. 'A star shall come forth out of Jacob, a comet arise from Israel, who shall smite Moab, Edom and Seir,' prophesied Balaam. 'The stars in their courses fought against Sisera,' proclaimed Deborah and Barak after their victory over Jabin's general. 'Jehovah,' cries Amos, 'made the Pleiades and Orion . . . and . . . makes Taurus rise after Capella and . . . set hard on the rising of the Vintager.'

According to one Christian view, the coming of Christ broke the control of the planets over human destiny. The Star of Bethlehem was a new one which changed the old inevitable order. But another view is that it was the constellation of Cassiopeia which, because every 300 years it produced an unusually bright star, was known to the ancients as 'The Woman with Child.' Furthermore, Cassiopeia was the presiding constellation of Syria–Palestine, and it was natural for the Magi – who were astrologers, not kings – to follow the sign which proclaimed to them that a woman of Palestine had brought forth a royal son.

A Christian astrologer could use this fact as an argument that his astral beliefs were sanctified by Scripture, though he would find little support from St Paul, who refers to the celestial powers as 'declining to their end' (I Cor. 2 : 6) and states that 'during our minority we were slaves to the elemental spirits of the universe' (Gal. 4 : 3) which are 'mean and beggarly' (verse 9). However much Cassiopeia may have celebrated the birth of Jesus, on his cross 'he discarded the cosmic powers and

Augurs divining by the entrails of a bull

authorities like a garment', leading them 'as captives in his triumphal procession'; and in Rev. 1 : 16 Christ is represented as holding 'the seven stars' in his hand.

The same contradictory outlook was apparent in early Christianity which was sometimes tolerant of, sometimes hostile to, astrology. The second-century *Clementine Recognitions* stated that God created the celestial bodies to be an indication of things past, present and future, and that Abraham, being an astrologer, recognized the creator from the stars. The author, Clement of Alexandria, was one of the first to acknowledge the problem of free will conflicting with fate determined by the stars, a question answered by Julius Firmicus Maternus about 335. Maternus, a convinced Christian, reconciling in his *Mathesis* astrology and Christianity, stated that the influence of the stars could always be resisted by the human will. Augustine and other hostile writers had an illogical best of both worlds by attacking astrology as being erroneous or, if ever right, by ascribing its accuracy to the devil.

During the recession of learning in the Dark Ages, astrology, like much other knowledge, all but disappeared. It was kept alive by the Muslims. In the eighth century the Caliph Al-Mansur founded a school of astrology in Baghdad, with the practical emphasis on methods of catching thieves, recovering lost possessions, and determining the best time to start an enterprise. A Sabian, Thebit ben Corat, influenced Christian Europe in a partly astrological work, which was twice translated into Latin, as were the books of Albumasar, an Arab of Baghdad (died *c.* 886). He distinguished between 'necessary' actions, which inevitably follow given conditions, and 'contingent' actions governed by factors which are incalculable and therefore debatable.

The Jews also played a small part in the survival of astrology. About AD 500 the *Sepher Yetsirah* ('Book of Creation') was written, one of the classics of the Jewish mystical system known as the Cabbala. The *Zohar* ('Book of Splendour'), dated variously from 900 to after 1280, was another. Both reveal a belief in celestial influence. By the use of a particular sign it was possible to evoke the force of a planet or its ruling angel, using their powers for material purposes.

The Star of Bethlehem

The re-emergence of astrology

When learning was revived in western Europe in the eleventh and twelfth centuries, Arabian astrological treatises were welcomed because of their Aristotelian flavour. Thomas Aquinas (c. 1226–74) stated what came to be the definitive Christian compromise with astrology. Since the stars influence human appetites, which few men can resist, their predictions are mostly correct; but those who are morally strong enough to control themselves can make the predictions wrong.

Contemporary with Aquinas were astrological schools in Muslim Spain and, once the great Christian scholar had established the respectability of astrology, chairs on the subject were founded at several Italian universities. Guido Bonatti wrote a famous astrological 'bible,' the *Liber Astronomicus*, which was circulated in translation throughout Europe, and in English as late as 1676 by William Lilly.

In the following centuries astrology–astronomy (for the two did not part company until the seventeenth century) increased in reputation until it reached its peak during the Renaissance. The interest in everything classical, including astrology closely linked with mythology, permeated to the mass of the people through printing. Famous scholars, such as the Italian Marsilio Ficino (1433–99), who published *Pimander*, an astrological treatise, and the Swiss alchemist Paracelsus (1493–1541) advanced the belief that man's inner nature corresponded to the universe; sun, moon, planets, stars, the void in which they dwell, all have their counterparts in man who can, however, resist their influence.

Some popes and many potentates favoured astrologers. Catherine de Medici patronized the famous Nostradamus, often credited with prophecies even more remarkable than those he actually produced in his *Centuries* of prophetic verses published in 1555, and Queen Elizabeth I had her court astrologer Dr John Dee. Even the discovery by Copernicus that the earth was not the centre of the universe but travelled round the sun, findings developed by Tycho Brahe, Kepler, and Galileo, whose perfection of the telescope revealed more of the heavens than man had ever known before, did not destroy astrology. In spite of strong condemnation by Pope Urban VIII in 1631, the most famous astrologer of the seventeenth century

'The moon and Jupiter meet in Sagittarius'. Page from an Islamic astrological treatise, *c.* 1250

was a priest, Placidus de Titis. His *Physiomathematica sive Coelestis Philosophia* earned him the title of the 'father of modern astrology.'

The age of reason

Although not destroyed, astrology was temporarily undermined by the new discoveries and practically disappeared in Europe. It was kept alive in England by men of considerable intellect such as William Lilly, who is said to have prophesied the Great Fire of London, Elias Ashmole, founder of the Ashmolean Museum, and John Flamsteed, the first astronomer-royal, who chose the date and hour for the founding of Greenwich Observatory by astrology. Even in England, however, it was almost destroyed in 1707 by ridicule. Under the pseudonym of 'Isaac Bickerstaff,' Jonathan Swift wrote a satire in which he forecast the death of Partridge, an almanac maker. (Almanacs were a vested interest of the Stationers' Company who from 1700 to 1890 profited handsomely from a

The Great Fire of London

monopoly of the publication of annual astronomical almanacs which maintained popular interest in astrology in Britain.) Partridge survived the fatal day, but 'Bickerstaff' published an account of his death which almost killed him and astrology with mockery.

The intellectual climate of the Age of Enlightenment drove superstition underground, and Sir William Herschel's discovery of the planet Uranus in 1781 dealt astrology a body-blow by destroying the mystic number seven. But this did not deter Ebenezer Sibley from publishing his *Science of Astrology* in 1790, reissued in 1812 and 1828, and an astro-medical text-book *The Key to Physick and the Occult Science*.

The nineteenth-century revival

At the same time that the Goddess of Reason was being enthroned in spirit throughout Europe (although only the revolutionaries in France actually enthroned her in person in Notre Dame Cathedral), there was beginning a reaction of faith

William Lilly

Madame Blavatsky, founder of the Theosophical Society

which expressed itself both in religious movements, such as the Methodist revival, and in occultism. The Austrian, Anton Mesmer, used hypnosis in a semi-scientific fashion, and the Frenchman Paul Christian in his *L'Homme Rouge des Tuileries* (1863) described seven spirits enthroned in the planets ruling thirty-six demons, corresponding to the decans, governing 360 intelligences, one for each degree of the zodiac – all these the agents of a universal intelligence. James Wilson's *A Complete Dictionary of Astrology* appeared in 1819, and in 1827 Robert Cross Smith under the name of Raphael, launched *The Prophetic Messenger*, still published today as *Raphael's Almanac, Prophetic Messenger and Weather Guide*.

In spite of the 1824 Vagrancy Act, which made fortune-telling by the stars a punishable offence, Richard James Morrison, a retired naval officer, lived the double life of a man about town and 'Zadkiel the Seer.' In 1829 he published *The*

Herald of Astrology, which subsequently appeared annually as *Zadkiel's Almanac*, and he was also the author of *A Grammar of Astrology* and the more technical *An Introduction to Astrology*. Other educated men, such as the Sheffield schoolmaster who published *W. J. Simmonite's Complete Arcana of Astral Philosophy* about 1848, and Richard Garnett (1835–1906), alias A. G. Trent, Keeper of Printed Books at the British Museum, maintained the astrological tradition unbroken in England.

An important event occurred in 1875 when Madame Blavatsky founded the Theosophical Society. There was at the time considerable interest in spiritualism, psychical research, and esoteric forms of religion, possibly as a reaction against growing scientific materialism. The Theosophical Society appealed to intellectuals, reviving interest in astrology, among

Raphael's Witch or The Oracle of the Future. 1831

other beliefs, not only in England but also on the Continent. Annie Besant, Madame Blavatsky's successor, ardently believed in astrology, and the Theosophical Society Astrological Lodge, founded in 1920, issues a quarterly journal *Astrology*, gives courses, and awards diplomas.

Meanwhile, in 1890, William Frederick Allen (1860–1917), under the name of Alan Leo, began *The Astrologer's Magazine* (later *Modern Astrology*) for a more popular market, and wrote manuals of instruction for laymen, as did 'Sepharial' (Walter Gorn Old), who produced over forty books on the subject. On the most popular level Foulsham's *Old Moore's Almanac*, with a continuous existence under different names since the eighteenth century and sold between the two World Wars for a penny, was widely hawked and bought. At the other extreme, the scholarly Faculty of Astrological Studies, founded in 1948, awards certificates, diplomas, scholarships, and medals to serious students of the subject.

The burning wreckage of the crashed R101

Astrology today

In France a revival in the early 1900s developed over thirty years into a widely popular movement catered for by several magazines, and the founding of the German branch of the Theosophical Society reawoke interest in astrology in that country. Elsbeth Ebertin began an annual prophetic almanac *Ein Blick in die Zukunft* ('A Glimpse into the Future') in 1917, and a startling prediction about Adolf Hitler in her 1924 issue made her widely known. German interest in astrology became intense during the 1920s and 1930s, although there is little evidence that Hitler trusted to it, as is often suggested. Astrology was, in fact, blamed for Rudolf Hess's flight to Britain in 1941 and banned as a result. However, it recovered quickly after the war.

A remarkable forecast, apparently of the R101 airship disaster, by R. H. Naylor in the *Sunday Express*, which published regular astrological articles from 1930 onwards, impressed the British public. Other newspapers introduced regular astral features and today there is scarcely a journal

without its starry column. Serious astrologers despise this 'pop' astrology as a debasement of their art, at best too generalized to be of value and at worst a possible danger to gullible readers who take it too seriously.

Elsewhere in the modern world astrology flourishes. The U.S. Theosophical Society gave an impetus to it, and a theosophist, Max Heindel, popularized it in a number of books. In 1926 Llewellyn George founded the National Astrological Association, which later became the American Federation of Astrologers. His was a scientific approach, but it is the popular brand of character delineation and forecasting the future that appeals most widely to Americans today, and ensures a wide sale for the many astrological books published.

India takes astrology very seriously. Only about a dozen learned astronomo-astrologers are allowed the supreme title of 'Jyotisha Pandit' and they issue an annual almanac called *Panchaga*. The police use astrologers in their work, and auspicious days are chosen for weddings, the launching of business ventures, and other important enterprises. Not all eastern countries favour astrology, for a bad forecast can cause panic among ordinary people. In the wide areas of the Communist world it is classed among superstitions to be eradicated.

Here we are concerned only with a summary of the history of astrology. Arguments for and against its truth will be given in the final chapter. How widely it is believed in the modern world it is impossible to say – some of its supporters maintain that one in five Americans, for example, has some faith in it. This is probably an exaggeration but, whatever the truth, there are few people today who do not know their zodiacal sign and who, if their eyes fall on 'What the Stars Foretell' in their daily paper, do not read the lines that concern them – and perhaps even allow themselves to be influenced a little by them.

(Opposite) The coronation of King Birendra Bir Bikram of Nepal in 1975 which took place according to the dictates of Brahmin astrological traditions

THE PLANETS

It should be recognized from the start that there are three types of astrology – 'pop', 'cook-book' and 'psychological' or 'intuitive'. 'Pop' is that generally found in newspapers and magazines, necessarily far too generalized to be of much use. 'Cook-book' is more serious. Its students, who are keen amateurs or professional astrologers, cast individual horoscopes using published ephemerides and a library of reference books in which every permutation and combination of planetary position are worked out. They may have an occasional shining success, but for the most part their interpretations will be uninspired and pedestrian. 'Intuitive' astrologers, however, are sensitives who translate their clients' charts with a psychic insight which gives their interpretations an indefinable 'plus' beyond the mere mechanics of the job. They cannot do their work without training, but no training can supply this sensitivity if it is not there. Opponents of astrology who nevertheless accept the existence of a psychic sense can argue that it is the intuition, not the stars, that reveals such truth as the horoscope shows.

Expressions such as 'the zodiac' have already been used without explanation in the text – their meanings will be found in the glossary on pages 124–5 – but here will be given a short explanation of the general system of astrological calculations.

The general system of calculation

The heavens are viewed as by an observer upon earth. To him the sun appears to move round the world from east to west following a path called the ecliptic. This path is the centre of a band called the zodiac, which is 16° wide (less than one-twentieth of the 360° of the circumference of the heavens) and within which all the planets, except Pluto, move. The zodiac is divided into twelve sections, each with its sign, originally the name of a constellation. However, astrologers are careful to point out that when they say that a subject is born under Pisces, this means the sign, not the constellation. The earth's movement makes each sign appear to move from east to west.

(Opposite) Astrological postage stamps from Burundi

The system is shown diagramatically as a wheel with hub, spokes and rim. The hub is the earth; the rim is the zodiac, moving in a clockwise direction from the east, shown in an astrological diagram on the *left*, to the west, like a tyre slipping, as it were, round a static wheel. The twelve spokes, called cusps, divide the wheel into twelve 'houses', which may vary in area according to different astrological systems, about whose merits their upholders debate keenly. For the sake of convenience they will here be treated as equal in size.

Within the houses the planets are placed according to their positions at the moment of an individual's birth, the launching of a ship, the making of a marriage, or the founding of a business. Each planet's influence may be strengthened or weakened by its position relative to the others, its 'aspects'.

A chart applies to a certain moment and a certain place. Knowledge of the exact moment, calculated according to certain rules, which will be given later, enables the astrologer to calculate which zodiacal sign is rising above the eastern horizon, shown at 'nine o'clock' on the chart. This sign is said to be 'in the ascendant'. The ascendant itself is the degree on the horoscope at the point marked M.C., standing for 'medium coeli' (mid-heaven).

Four influences have to be plotted and interpreted. First is that of the 'sun sign', that is, the sign of the zodiac in which the sun is at the time of the chart. Second are shown the houses, which have the same positions on all horoscopes, numbered as on the diagram (opposite), the first concerned with childhood, the second with possessions, and so on. Third come the planets, which strongly influence the houses in which they are placed, so that a maleficent planet in the twelfth house, which includes sorrow among its concerns, might indicate a life of tragedy whereas a 'benefic' might cancel out much sadness. Fourth are the effects of the aspects which may very greatly modify the influences of individual planets.

All these forces have to be studied, balanced and interpreted. The number of possible permutations is enormous and further complicated by disagreement over methods of interpretation by astrologers, who are, however, no more to be condemned for this than scientists who explain facts by different theories. It is for this reason that the 'cook-books' exist. As logarithm tables

The zodiacal system. For the houses (numbered) see pp. 84–87. For the sign meanings, see pp. 54–55

help the mathematician in his calculations, so astrological reference books summarize for the working astrologer the positions of the heavenly bodies at given times and their interpretations.

It must be realized, therefore, that the following summary of the planets' characteristics can only be approximate. Not only are they modified by other planets but they have changed from age to age, and the astrologers of any one age do not always agree in their interpretation.

The sun

The sun, usually beneficent, is the male principle of father-hood, universal (some would say symbolic of the father-hood of God) and particular, the all-pervading creative power of nature. Some of its characteristics are authority, as the head of its own system of planets, self-integration, wholeness of being, generative and vitalizing power, positiveness and forcefulness. The native (astrologically the subject of a horoscope) with the sun prominent in his chart, may be intellectual, successful and a natural leader, or, negatively, intolerant, arrogant, ostentatious and bombastic, disguising underlying weakness. The sun represents his career to a man, her menfolk to a woman, and its position in the zodiac on the birth-chart often, though not always, determines the native's zodiacal type.

Physiologically the sun affects the whole physical body in energizing it through the heart. As the sun pulsates heat, warmth and energy to its universe, so the heart pumps the blood conveying these elements of life to the body. The sun also controls the thymus gland which regulates the body's rate of growth, a parallel process to the sun's control of the growth of crops and all living things on earth (too much or too little sun can both bring disaster).

Psychically the sun symbolizes spiritual energy in the individual and within the 'collective unconscious', the name C. G. Jung gives to that inherited psychic material present in us which links us with all mankind. The sun's symbol is a point within a circle, ⊙ the circle representing divine spirit and completeness, the point the nucleus or seed of the potential individual.

Each planet has a special relationship with one or more zodiacal signs and houses. The sun's is Leo, its house the fifth, its day Sunday and its best hours the first, eighth, fifteenth and twenty-second.

The moon

The Babylonians regarded the moon as male, but in modern astrological thought its feminine qualities predominate. Delicate feeling, the sensitiveness of the inner nature, intelligence evolving spirit as it assimilates and reflects on

experience, affection (especially in the home), receptiveness, impressionability, changes of mind, moodiness, the following of fashion in taste and thought, impulsiveness, restlessness, placidity, passivity, timidity, fantasy and a dreamy disposition, sometimes fierce pride in her feminine qualities in a woman – all are characteristics of the lunar native. The fact that some of them are contradictory indicates the native's innate inconsistency, explained astrologically by the double pull of the sun (spirit) and the earth (matter). But inconsistency does not always appear. Since the moon also indicates a subject's outward manner, the conjunction of moon and sun presents a native who is exactly what he appears to be. If their influences are opposed, they suggest a character who sees himself as one type while others see him as different, even opposite. A many-aspected moon shows a man who suits his behaviour to his company, whereas a single-aspected one results in consistent conduct. A prominently placed moon may cause its subject to choose a profession which brings him to public attention in a humble or distinguished capacity.

The moon is commonly associated in thought with love and water. Lunar love is, however, spiritual and non-sexual, associated with cold chastity or the affection felt for sister by brother or for son by mother. The obvious influence of the moon on the tides makes it the symbol of change and motion, and it governs 'those who go down to the sea in ships, that do business in great waters'.

Rhythm is characteristic of the moon. It has much to do with female rhythm, the sidereal lunar month corresponding to the menstrual cycle and the waxing moon being symbolic of pregnancy. Its cycle portrays the physical phases of life, growth and decay, and the conjunction of sun and new moon indicates copulation, the synodic month (the period between two moons) deriving its name from the Greek *synodos* ('copulation'). The moon is supposed especially to influence plant growth.

Physiologically the moon has to do with the body-fluids in the digestive and lymphatic systems which nourish, protect and lubricate, and it therefore controls the stomach, womb, ovaries, breasts and pancreas (a faulty pancreas can give rise to emotional instability). It also affects the sympathetic nervous system which influences the native's emotional character.

Psychically, the moon links past and present, its subjects sometimes looking nostalgically backwards, but, if well balanced, using memories of past experience as a springboard for future action. Through its establishment of physical and mental rhythms, it forms habit-patterns arising out of the ebb and flow of sensation and the emotional response to it. The

Lunar native has a strong sense of family and, often, patriotism, but runs the risk of developing a 'mother-complex'. The moon's sign is Cancer, appropriately a water-sign, and its hour is the fourth. Its symbol is an incomplete circle, ☽, representing mind both conscious and unconscious, its day Monday, its best hours the second, ninth, sixteenth and twenty-third.

37

Mercury

Mercury, smallest of the planets, nearest to the sun, with greater lineal speed and shortest sidereal period, was in mythology the nimble messenger of the gods. Its smallness and closeness to its 'parent' make it the planet of childhood and youth, with corresponding characteristics. It is associated with the childish vices of lying, fraud and theft (Mercury was the patron god of thieves) and the childlike qualities of innocence and charm. The qualities of youth also belong to it – sprightliness, volatility, changeability and restlessness. To be 'mercurial' in temperament may be good or bad. For the Mercurian, with his ready wit, eloquence, dashing intuition, intelligence, intellectualism, rationalism, brilliance, good memory and artistic ability, may be outstanding in almost any educational field. Capable of great learning, greedy for knowledge, objective and able to remain uninvolved, he enjoys communicating his erudition to others as professor, teacher or journalist. A spokesman for the rights of others, he could be a politician or trades union official. He could be a doctor, a great traveller and road-maker, efficient in commerce and business, an expert in communication systems, inventive and technically skilled in carpentry and engineering.

But his faults match his capabilities. He can be subtle, cunning, shallow, glib, open to error, calculating, rashly impetuous, frivolous, slippery, capricious – a spiritual chameleon. Rather than admit ignorance, he will answer a question incorrectly. It has been said that not all Mercurians are plausible rogues but a plausible rogue may very likely be a Mercurian. So they make efficient confidence tricksters and criminals. Love for the Mercurian is 'games people play' – his head governs his heart, he is fickle and cold and marries with mental reservations, and he may be a masochist. Even in his positive attributes, his learning may be wide rather than deep, his art superficial and lacking in seriousness.

Physically, Mercury governs the central nervous system, the brain (its conscious and subconscious sides corresponding to Mercury's one side always exposed to the sun, its other always facing away from it) as the seat of reason, logic, consciousness and the will, and the interpreter of sensations and the unconscious, and the thyroid which controls, among other

things, movement, volatility, nervous reaction, physical and mental growth and critical functional changes during life.

Mercury's signs are Gemini and Virgo, its houses the third and sixth, its day Wednesday, its hours the fourth, eleventh and eighteenth. Its symbol ☿ is a half-circle (human mind and spirit) over a circle (completeness, divine spirit) and a cross (matter).

Venus

Venus, the only planet named after a female deity, originally a goddess of spring and therefore connected with fertility and new life, is associated with sexual love (though not necessarily the physical aspect of sex). Friendship, affection, personal relationships, motherhood, beauty, physical attractiveness, elegance, love of beautiful things, the arts, harmony, reconciliation, peace, pleasure, voluptuousness – all these are her province. Her natives may be witty, pure and (surprisingly!) faithful, fond of dancing and haters of evil, but will prefer the experience of the senses to rationalized judgement.

Venus represents the feminine in both sexes. The male Venusian may be under the thumbs of his womenfolk or have feminine qualities himself. These need not be despicable – many extremely civilized men show their Venusian natures in their warmth, sympathy, physical grace and attractiveness. They are creative, artistic, aesthetic, loving beauty, especially in music. They need to receive affectionate appreciation as well as to give it. Both sexes are tactful and contented, valuing cooperation and unity of purpose with their partners. They appreciate most of all harmony in personal relationships and strive always to eradicate roughness and discordance. They are good at business, for Venus is associated with good fortune and the ability to make money.

Negatively, Venusians may be yielding, passive, timorous, effeminate, promiscuously and sordidly amorous, and dull. They may be unutterably lonely. Venus is markedly affected by other planets. Her conjunction with Saturn and Mercury indicates death by poison, the woman's weapon, or female domination. Her conjunction with the sun makes a man effeminate; square to Saturn indicates selfishness; in Gemini shows fickleness, even promiscuity; in Taurus indicates one slow to choose a spouse yet steadfast and reliable, though possessive, when he does; and in Scorpio shows an intensely passionately sexual lover.

Physiologically, Venusians risk gastric troubles through their fondness for spicy foods and genital diseases because of their sexual natures. The Venus principle of unity leads it to govern the parathyroids which, through their control of calcium content, build the framework of the skeleton, and to

rule the lumbar region.

Venus' symbol, ♀, a circle (completeness, divine spirit) above a cross (matter) also normally indicates feminine gender. The planet is associated with Taurus, Libra and the second and seventh houses. Her day is Friday, her hours the seventh, thirteenth and nineteenth.

Mars

If the influence of Mars, 'the rogue male' of the planets, were unadulterated, it would produce vile characters ranging from bully to coward. The redness of the physical planet, associated by the Babylonians with carnage, plague and disaster, but by the Romans originally with protection against pests, storms and droughts, portrays danger, fire, blood and anger. Without counterbalancing influences a native of Mars could be aggressive, violent, malevolent, mischievous, cruel, bloody, extravagant, boisterous, ruffianly, drunken, rapacious, a vandal, or brutally lustful. In a woman's horoscope, Mars represents male influence, especially a husband's. But other influences are, fortunately, rarely missing, and the native's vices are matched by corresponding virtues. Though impatient, hasty, excitable and easily angered, he is as easily appeased. He is self-assertive but enterprising, thorough, tirelessly energetic, enjoying work for its own sake. He can be noble, warlike, imperial, utterly fearless, yet his boldness and impulsiveness do not make him take unnecessary risks. Although a versatile pioneer with the initiative to change existing institutions, he likes to move in familiar paths, for he is neither subtle, deep nor artistic, and lacks the imagination to attempt the unusual. He must be taken at face value, rough, brusque and unrefined in manner though he may be. But Mars gives scholars the persistence to persevere in tedious research, and martyrs the tenacity to hold to their convictions in spite of the threat of terrible deaths. Natives can be athletes, barbers, butchers, metal-workers, policemen and soldiers, but may be scholars and, as Mars represents the masculinity principle, are men in their capacities as fathers and husbands.

Mars governs the muscles and urogenital systems, sex glands, adrenals, sympathetic nervous system, red blood corpuscles and, partly, the kidneys. He musters the resistance of the body against disease and is the master of energy and fluids flowing out from the centre. The adrenals rouse him to fight and stimulate self-defence and sex-activity. Martian natives are subject to red, hot ills – inflammation, fevers, burns, scalds, and wounds from blood-letting instruments.

The symbol for Mars is that used in biology for the male, ♂, the cross (matter), sometimes represented by an arrow

· MARS ·

(initiative and objectivity), over the circle (divine spirit). Mars' zodiac connections are Aries and Scorpio, his houses the first and eighth, his day Tuesday, and his hours the third, tenth, seventeenth and twenty-fourth.

Jupiter

The largest planet, Jupiter, has been regarded as the most beneficent ever since astrology began. His natives are benevolent, patriarchal people, upholding the best in the status quo in the realm of law, morals and religion. Mentally, they are profound, far-reaching thinkers, philosophers who use their experience of life to develop a consciousness beyond mundane things. They could be judges upholding law and the established order, inspired by ideals of guarding the helpless and tempering justice with mercy and equity. In any profession they are likely to be outstanding, leaders who achieve high position and wealth, in clubs and societies as well as in business and commerce. They are dignified, natural rulers, often good-looking, or at least imposing with an impressive manner, expecting reverence and respect as their due. Since they are conventional in thought, dress and behaviour, they like things as they are.

But they are not selfish. They are generous, affable, humorous, expansive and friendly – 'jovial' is Jupiter's adjective. They have a social conscience, using their power to protect, heal, console, preserve and encourage. Their private conscience urges them to expand their capabilities. They are ambitious to understand life, attain maturity, and recognize. and eradicate their weaknesses. Optimistic and sometimes happy-go-lucky, if they do meet bad fortune they face it courageously, carrying on in hopeless positions and with greater tenacity than most. They may inspire irritation in the young, for they are middle-aged in outlook, inclined to stoutness, though usually healthy.

An ill-aspected Jupiter may influence the native to be 'larger than life,' bombastic, a boaster, a procrastinator, with tendencies to exaggeration, extravagance and conceit.

Physically Jupiter governs the liver, the pituitary gland, the fat of the body and its general expansion, protection and healing, so that recovery of health after illness is its province. The liver purifies the blood of poisons and bacteria. The jolly fat man is a jovial type, with his well-larded body, but such fat may predispose to ill-health even though making its possessor 'a fine figure of a man'. The pituitary gland controls hormone production and performs a healing harmonizing function.

· IVPITER ·

Jupiter's symbol, ♃, is the half-circle (mind and human spirit) rising above the cross (matter), symbolizing spirit rising from and transcending experience. The planet is associated with positive masculine Sagittarius and negative feminine Pisces, and the ninth and twelfth houses. Thursday is Jupiter's day and his best hours the fifth, twelfth and nineteenth.

Saturn

If Mercury be taken as the planet of youth and Jupiter as that of middle age, then Saturn is the patron of the shrunk-shanked dotard. But such a picture is not altogether fair. Saturnian qualities are necessary in any well-balanced human, though they are pedestrian and, in excess, unpleasant and even evil.

The Saturnian, often dark and grave in appearance, is self-disciplined, controlled, cautious, responsible, capable of hard work and great concentration, mature, sober, wise, discreet, practical, resourceful. He plans for the future, trying to forearm himself against the unexpected, often according to a rigorous time-table, so he is happiest in routine work which enables him to plan ahead, especially if it provides steady advancement and a pension at the end. He feels difficulties keenly but endures them patiently. As he is naturally slow, his skills and talents may develop late. Business, politics, the civil service, the church, the army, building, architecture, civil engineering, contemplative occupations, would all suit him, provided he were not required to make decisions suddenly nor exert flamboyant and inspiring leadership in crises.

A 'good' Saturnian is not necessarily happy. Although possessing the 'saturnine' humour which is often the most intellectual, his concern with self-discipline may make him aware of his shortcomings. He may see himself as an inadequate, inhibited and lonely failure, such thoughts increasing his tendency to dourness, melancholy and suspicion. He may be saved by his wife, whom he will care and provide for with scrupulous loyalty, and she, if a Saturnian, will provide economically and carefully for him.

At their best, Saturnian qualities, however worthy, are dull. But Saturn is the planet of the worst. Limitation, depression, ill-fortune, separation, sense of loss, especially bereavement by death, fear, sorrow, suffering, hardship, the ills of old age, all come under its sway. The character defects of emotional coldness, selfishness, miserliness, malevolence and downright cruelty may mar the native of Saturn.

Physiologically, Saturn governs the bones, skin and teeth, among other parts of the body, imposing a necessary rigidity upon it. In skeleton and skull it provides emblems of death and brings about death itself by the gradual hardening, wearing out

and slowing down of the system, increasingly dry.

Its symbol, $\hbar$ is the cross (matter) over the half-circle (mind, human spirit), indicating the limitation of mind and spirit by the grossness of the physical clay. Saturn's zodiacal signs are Capricorn and Aquarius, its houses the tenth and eleventh, its day Saturday and its best hours the seventh, fourteenth and twenty-first.

47

Uranus

Because Uranus takes so long to traverse the circle of the zodiac, it, with its more recently discovered brothers, Neptune and Pluto, is thought to influence generations rather than individual lives. Some astrologers believe that it is only when a new planet becomes known that it makes any impact upon human affairs. The influence of Uranus, therefore, is seen in the American, French and Industrial Revolutions, and in the violent changes and new developments of the past two centuries, for it is the planet of sudden awakening and the urge for freedom expressed in rebellion. In the individual it produces the drive to deviate from the normal, giving him an original, versatile, inventive, independent mind, impatient of old systems and accepted ideas, free in expression and behaviour, especially sexually and morally. So unconventional a spirit may possess intuition, insight, creative inspiration and flashes of genius leading to further advances in knowledge, especially scientific and technological, and, in this present age when men are aware of the problems of all other nations, altruism and a practical sense of brotherhood.

The negative aspects of Uranian free-thinking are rebellion rather than reform, irresponsibility, violent eccentricity, and perverted and depraved fanaticism. As the planet is also said to govern transmutation, magic and the occult, astrologers call themselves 'children of Uranus'.

The planet is associated physiologically with the sympathetic nervous system and its bad aspects cause illnesses which resemble sudden revolutions – nervous breakdowns, hysteria, spasms, cramps, paralysis, palpitations and instability arising from the change of life. Homosexuality and sexual perversion are also said to be associated with it.

The planet's sign ♅ was originally the H of Herschel, its discoverer, surmounting a circle, and reminds some observers amusingly of a television aerial, one of the technological wonders of our age. It is associated with Aquarius and the eleventh house, and, like Neptune and Pluto, has no day assigned to it.

Uranus

Neptune

When Neptune was discovered in 1846, there was transferred to it from the moon the government of the seas and all liquids. It also controls a considerable province of human activity although it takes nearly fifteen years to traverse a single sign of the zodiac and can therefore hardly affect individuals. Its natives are those who seek to tap spiritual energies beyond the physical, and astrologers point out that its discovery was almost contemporary with the birth of modern spiritualism and a reawakened interest in the occult.

Psychics, sensitives, mediums, magicians, religious visionaries, reformers, mystics and idealistic humanists with their subtle, susceptible, unworldly natures, are 'children of Neptune', with musicians, artists and writers. An extreme sensitivity and physical and mental impressionability may make them excessively impractical, vague, confused and chaotic in their daily lives. Worse than this, the problems of life and horrors of much of the news may drive them into a desire to escape reality, either by distorting it grossly in romantic or sensational fantasies in which they deceive themselves as well as attempt to deceive others, or by day-dreaming intensified little by little into hallucination. In extreme cases they may induce escape by sedatives, drugs and alcohol or may indulge their neuroses by sexual orgies and perversions, all these being roads to disintegration of the personality, despair and suicide, often by poison or gas. Neptune governs psychic conditions such as mesmerism, hypnotism and trance, and inculcates a love of the sea which carries a risk of death by drowning.

Physiologically it has to do with the thalamus, that part of the brain controlling the optic and aural nerves and rhythms of growth, the spinal canal and some nervous and mental processes. Within its province are mysterious illnesses, such as mental and emotional disturbances, neuroses, obsessional fears, hysteria and insanity.

The trident Ψ is Neptune's sign, the half-circle of the human mind or spirit transcending the cross of matter. Its zodiacal sign is Pisces and it is connected with the twelfth house.

Neptune

Pluto

Pluto's motto could be 'Mors ianua vitae' ('Death the gateway to life') for its principle is renewal through elimination. Discovered only in 1930, it takes 248 years to circle the sun and zodiac. It is regarded as a planet of destruction (Pluto was god of death and the underworld), but not hopelessly so, for future growth rises out of the destruction or often violent transformation of the past. Astrologers point out that Pluto's discovery was almost contemporary with that of atomic power culminating in the bomb, economic depression, the climax of domestic racketeering and gangsterism followed by international gangsterism in the form of dictatorships, the rise of colossal international enterprises and cartels in business and of superpowers in politics, and mass hysteria like the Nuremberg rallies.

Larger-than-life emphasis is the mark of Pluto – it makes everything better or worse than it would normally be. If prominent in the chart of an individual, it makes him a striking personality for good or ill, the planet's eccentric orbit suggesting the heights or depths to which man can rise or fall. The Plutonian is said to be a staunch home-lover needing a firm base from which to launch his highly individual career in which he will prefer, if possible, to strike out on his own.

Within the personality Pluto symbolizes the limits of the present state of man's consciousness and what lies beyond it – those unknown powers and activities deep in the subconscious which sometimes result in parapsychological phenomena, sometimes in deep-seated neuroses. These need to be revealed, perhaps by psycho-analysis, and sublimated so that the patient may make a new beginning towards wholeness, for Pluto is the planet of the Whole Self battling against individual discordancies. These left unchanged in the subconscious could lead later to outbreaks of violent neurosis, even to lunacy.

Physiologically Pluto is concerned with the creative and regenerative processes, cell-formation, and reproductive functions in their widest sense. Some astrologers assign to it Scorpio and the eighth house. Its symbol, $\underline{P}$, represents the initials of Percival Lowell who calculated Pluto's position before its discovery, and could also represent the circle of the human mind connected to the level of the subconscious or even those forces below and beyond it.

Pluto

THE SIGNS OF THE ZODIAC

The planets represent basic characteristics which are presumably independent of man's existence. If humankind were to destroy itself tomorrow by a nuclear war, the sun would continue to transmit its light and heat, the phases of the moon would endure in their calm succession and the planets would transmit their influence even if there were nobody to affect. The bridge between the planets and man, which translates their basic principles into human psychological types is the zodiac, and in this chapter the characteristics of each sign will be summarized.

As with the planets so with the signs; there are no absolutes. Every human being is different because no man or woman is born at exactly the same time in exactly the same place under exactly the same stars. So the characteristics of the signs which are listed below are approximate and subject to the many influences outlined in the previous chapter.

In addition to their individual characteristics, planets are classified as being positive (masculine) or negative (feminine), and under the four elements, fire, air, earth and water (known as the triplicities, because there are three planets to each element), and as cardinal, fixed or mutable (the quadruplicities, there being four signs to each division). Positive signs are spontaneous and self-expressive, negative signs withdrawn and passive. Fire is lively and aggressive; earth matter-of-fact and controlled; air lively in mind and fluent in expression of every kind; water sensitive and intuitive. The cardinal quality is initiative, the fixed is steadfastness, the mutable is changeableness and adaptability.

The signs in their order from first to twelfth with their dates, classifications and symbols are:

First: Aries (the Ram). 21 March to 20 April. Positive. Fire. Cardinal. Ruler, Mars. ♈

Second: Taurus (the Bull). 21 April to 20 May. Negative. Earth. Fixed. Ruler, Venus. ♉

Third: Gemini (the Twins). 21 May to 21 June. Positive. Air. Mutable. Ruler, Mercury. ♊

Fourth: Cancer (the Crab). 22 June to 22 July. Negative. Water. Cardinal. Ruler, the moon. ♋

Fifth: Leo (the Lion). 23 July to 22 August. Positive. Fire. Fixed. Ruler, the sun. ♌

Sixth: Virgo (the Virgin). 23 August to 22 September. Negative. Earth. Mutable. Ruler, Mercury. ♍

Seventh: Libra (the Scales). 23 September to 22 October. Positive. Air. Cardinal. Ruler, Venus. ♎

Eighth: Scorpio (the Scorpion). 23 October to 22 November. Negative. Water. Fixed. Ruler, Mars. ♏

Ninth: Sagittarius (the Archer). 23 November to 22 December. Positive. Air. Mutable. Ruler, Jupiter. ♐

Tenth: Capricorn (the Goat). 23 December to 20 January. Negative. Earth. Cardinal. Ruler, Saturn. ♑

Eleventh: Aquarius (the Water Carrier). 21 January to 19 February. Positive. Air. Fixed. Ruler, formerly Saturn, now Uranus. ♒

Twelfth: Pisces (the Fish). 20 February to 20 March. Negative. Water. Mutable. Rulers, Jupiter and Neptune. ♓

Students will find that different authorities give slightly different dates for some of these signs, and natives born on or near the cusps may partake of the characteristics of either or both of two neighbouring signs.

Aries

Arietans are courageous leaders, energetic, restless, aggressive pioneers, inspired by ambition, adventurousness, impulsiveness, love of freedom, new ideas and a desire for quick results. They welcome challenges and enjoy overcoming difficulties. In their personal relationships they are frank, candid and direct, and make enthusiastic and generous friends, though they are often too impulsive. They are also argumentative, quick-tempered, impatient, easily offended, sensitive themselves while thoughtlessly insensitive to others. They can be brusque, rude, bullying and even brutal. Their genuine concern for people is balanced by their manipulation of them for their own purposes as leaders. They are passionate but fastidious lovers, and the intensity of their sex drive can lead them into early imprudent marriages which, since they have little loyalty and tenacity and love change, often end in shipwreck.

Mentally they are quickwitted, objective and intellectual but can be bigoted. They lack both thoroughness and the ability to foresee difficulties, and they are foolhardy and over-optimistic. A tendency to exaggerate plus a strong imagination sometimes leads them into downright lies which they believe themselves. Other faults are self-centredness and selfishness, sometimes expressing themselves in greed, resentment if they are not given what they consider their due, violence and lack of moderation in action and expression, with unwillingness to obey or submit. This last characteristic makes them good champions of last-ditch causes. The exhausting pace at which they burn themselves out each day makes it hard for them to rise in the morning, but this is balanced by their conviction that punctuality is the politeness of leaders of men such as themselves. They make good politicians, soldiers, captains of industry, doctors, explorers, farmers, climbers and athletes, provided they can discipline themselves. Their greatest need is an iron self-control.

Aries governs the head physiologically, and its natives have a tendency to head injuries and illnesses such as migraine, neuralgia and sunstroke. Because of impulsiveness, lack of planning and courage spilling over into rashness, Arietans are prone to accident and physical injury.

57

Taurus

Taureans combine the qualities of the bull with those of their ruling planet, Venus, and this explains some apparent inconsistencies. Physically they can be hefty and clodhopping, yet often majestically good-looking. Emotionally they are affectionate, generous and faithful. In spite of sensual self-consciousness and more than average amorousness, they are thoughtful, kind, undemanding, constant, sexually straightforward, and home-loving. Although perhaps over-possessive, they are good citizens with a sense of material values and respect for property which makes them sometimes too conservative and foolishly hostile to any change. At work they are industrious, not afraid of dirt, reliable, practical and methodical, but they can be lazy and disinclined to exercise.

Positive Taureans may be ambitious within a framework of obedience to superiors, often creative and good founders of enterprises. They are productive, their rewards the result of their own work, not of others'. They work best in secure routine positions of trust and responsibility with a pension in view, where their methodical nature is not faced with urgency and change. They have a horror of debt which drives them as powerfully as love for their family. They are good at handicrafts and can flourish in many trades – building, farming, banking, bureaucracy, industry, architecture, surveying, accountancy, auctioneering, insurance, education, music and sculpture – and make ideal trustees or guardians. They have a strong aesthetic sense, enjoying beauty, music and art, for which they may have a flair, and avoiding ugliness. Allied to this is a love of pleasure, good food, luxury and comfort which, over-indulged, can lead them into covetousness and grossness. Their religious faith, sometimes unconventional, is nevertheless often strong. Their minds are keen-witted and practical rather than intellectual, their opinions fixed, following accepted and reliable patterns, sometimes too slavishly.

They can be obstinately and exasperatingly stolid and self-righteous, though in the main they are modest, gentle, even-tempered and good-natured and avoid ill-feeling. When pushed too far, they can explode into ferocious anger as unexpected as their occasional humour and sense of fun. But in

the main they are reliable and steadfast, wise, just, firm, unshaken in the face of daunting difficulties. Their vices are their virtues in extreme, for they can become unoriginal bores, over-cautious, stodgy, rigid, stuck in a self-centred rut, argumentative and nursing a sense of injury. They are inclined to brood, and for all their sterling qualities need someone to say 'well done' to them.

As Taurus governs the throat and neck, his natives need to beware of throat infections and goitre. They are also open to problems of overweight and diseases of the genitals and womb.

Gemini

The keys to the understanding of Geminians are their twin natures and their connection with Mercury, planet of childhood and youth. The former makes them versatile, adaptable and able to see both sides of a question, but also restless, vacillating, inconsistent and two-faced, dilettantes failing through losing themselves in too many projects. Their connection with Mercury makes them youthful in character and appearance, sometimes even childish, so that, like children, they demand attention, admiration and the spending of time, energy and money on them. Moreover, they throw tantrums if they don't get them. Life is a game which must always be novel, entertaining and exciting, free of routine and labour.

Their emotional natures are likewise inconsistent, the key to them being that Geminians take nothing, not even themselves, seriously. They can be kind, courteous, affectionate, generous and thoughtful towards the poor and suffering. But in love they are light-hearted, cool, superficial, fickle, flirtatious, unimaginative, valuing the excitement of the chase, intrigue, novelty and experiment, more than permanent relationships. Never dull and with playfulness just under the surface, they can quixotically champion causes, winning a reputation for devotion and heroism through taking danger no more seriously than anything else. But they can be hard, egoistical, irritable, worriers, nervously excitable, withdrawn, discontented, uncertain of themselves and weak-willed.

Fortunately, their keen, intuitive intelligence, grasping almost everything easily, usually helps them to control their duality and to mature. Mentally agile and energetic, they have voracious appetites for learning from their schooldays onwards. They manipulate language skilfully in speech and writing and can be brilliant conversationalists, debaters, orators, preachers, teachers, barristers, authors, poets and journalists. Their dispassionate, logical, rational, often amoral minds make them the enemies of hazy sentimental thought, enabling them to become mathematicians, doctors and astronomers. They are sometimes outstanding in music, painting and sculpture. There is scarcely anything requiring intelligence and dexterity which Geminians cannot do if their

faculties are fully stretched, including research into the occult, in spite of their natural scepticism. Negatively, they can become prattlers, flowery orators and preachers without substance, factious, liars, cheats, boasters, spivs, thieves and confidence tricksters, and adepts in the black arts.

Gemini governs the lungs, nervous system, hands and arms (Geminians are great gesticulators) and its natives must beware of pulmonary illnesses, nervous diseases and exhaustion.

Cancer

It is difficult to give Cancerians a clear-cut character. They range from timid and dull to scintillating and brilliant. The famous born under Cancer have been many and varied.

Outwardly thick-skinned, uncompromising and unemotional, Cancerians are inwardly sensitive to other people, art, literature and psychic influences. Mentally, they are equally a mixture of tough and soft. Shrewdness, intuition, a retentive memory, prudence, philosophical profundity of thought verging on inspiration, are balanced by sympathy, imagination, artistic ability, emotionalism, even sentimentality, and romanticism. Their loving is not sentimental, however, but tenaciously loyal. The Cancerian male, though open to sensual stimulation, is the protector and nourisher of his family, which he needs as a secure base to which he can retire when he needs to restore his self-confidence; the Cancerian woman is strongly maternal. Both love unreservedly, giving much and asking little in return, and since they live intensely in the past and future as well as in the present, unrequited love, even if apparently conquered, may continue to influence them. The negative side of the Cancerians' affection, which allows them to be easily influenced by those they love and admire, is a clannishness and patriotism which makes them cold and suspicious towards outsiders.

In their daily lives, they are determined, intuitive, tenacious and purposeful. But they are susceptible to many faults. They may be sensual, unstable, changeable in opinions and loyalties, tactless, easily corrupted, moody, difficult and devious. In spite of ambition they may frequently change occupations, and they may be convincing romanticizers, inclined to self-pity, untidy, easily flattered, brooding on insults and suffering from an inferiority complex. They float with the popular tide, and this makes them good writers and journalists, interested in what people think, and able to judge what they can safely be told.

Other work suitable for the Cancerian is public affairs and anything involving looking after others from nursing to catering. They have some ability for trade and business, with a practical sense of value and economy. At their best, they can inspire their generation, especially its youth, by their idealism, provided they can reconcile the inner conflict of their outgoing urge with their indrawn reserve.

Physiologically, Cancer governs the breasts, female reproductive system and stomach, giving a tendency to digestive and womb troubles, dropsy and breast disorders.

Leo

Leos are natural leaders, uncomplicated, outgoing and outspoken, their spontaneous, generous, warm-hearted enthusiasm, loyalty to their causes and personal magnetism commanding loyalty in others. Practical, cheerful, humane, philosophical and spiritual, they are usually powerful for good. Their breadth of mind, strength of intelligence, courage, creativeness (they are the most spontaneously creative of the zodiacal types), untrammelled by doubt, lead them to expect success in any undertaking. They are magnanimous, dignified and attractive personalities, knowing exactly what they want and using all their energy, creativeness and resolution to achieve it. Everything they do is big and they delegate details of their grandiose schemes to underlings. They love pleasure, beauty and luxury and have a strong sense of drama.

They are so easily attracted to the opposite sex that they can scarcely avoid inconstancy and can be intensely sexual and dissolute. Failed marriages often follow numerous unfortunate love-affairs. They are sincere and generous to their lovers while love lasts, but too self-centred, overbearing and greedy for flattery to relate easily and harmoniously to their partners. They can be attached to their homes so long as these are run for their benefit, but demand service while incapable of giving it. In their choice of friends, exaggerated faith in humanity may lead to blunders, emphasized by favouritism.

Their faults are those of excess – arrogance, overweening conceit, bombast and pomposity. Snobbery makes them intolerant, dogmatic and prejudiced, but they are not above borrowing immoderately from any inferior willing to lend. Their hasty temper, impetuosity, greed for power and autocratic, patronizing behaviour match the sensuousness and emotionalism in which they over-indulge. Suspicious of rivals, they are not above using lies, trickery and cunning to outwit them. But their generosity, wisdom and the satisfaction of accustomed success usually control the self-assertive element. Leos are consequently beneficent influences in their professions, in which they will find 'room at the top' as managers, directors, chairmen, organizers, overseers and cabinet ministers. If artistically inclined, they will make their marks as stars on the stage, as maestros in the world of music, and as

Academicians at least in artistic circles.

Leo's physiological province is the heart, spine and back, and his natives are therefore susceptible to cardiac and spinal complaints.

Virgo

Virgo, the only female zodiacal sign, has been likened to a potentially creative girl, delicately lovely, with an enquiring mind. Male Virgoans may look effeminate but are not, and both sexes have dignity and considerable charm. Quiet, unassuming, undemonstrative, shrinking from close relationships, concealing their real selves, making few and superficial friendships, they are reputed to be cold and sometimes are, for all their outward cheerfulness and agreeableness. But in spite of their conventional, refined and even aristocratic attitude, they can be genuinely affectionate and good family members, although their love-making is a perfection of technique rather than an expression of desire. They are witty, sensible, discreet, well-spoken, practical, understanding other people's problems and never betraying confidences, though they are apt to interfere in their desire to help. Intellectually they are shrewd, studious and teachable, ingenious and skilful with their hands, with potential abilities in the arts, sciences and languages, which they use clearly, concisely and formally.

Their minds are logical, analytical and critical and so meticulous in detail that they may neglect larger issues. They conscientiously aspire to perfection but, though thorough and hardworking, are easily discouraged. They suspect abstract ideas and are realistic and exact to the point of pedantry. They readily assimilate new ideas but are cautious, conserving what is valuable in the past, and are careful with money. They love country life provided it does not upset their fondness for hygiene and cleanliness, for they are fastidious, female Virgoans particularly in dress, in which they may lead the fashion. Their faults are the extremes of their virtues, modesty becoming spinsterishness; criticism carping and nagging; concern for detail turning into over-specialization. There is also indecision in wider issues and an enlarging of molehills into mountains; prudence into guile; and carefulness into worry and hypochondria.

Virgoans' work should include routine, attention to detail and opportunity for service. They may make good doctors, nurses, psychologists, teachers, accountants, secretaries, statisticians, technologists, analytical scientists, inspectors, musicians, historians, public speakers, critics, editors and

writers, especially of such works as dictionaries and en-cyclopaedias.

Physiologically, Virgo controls the abdomen, intestines, spleen and central nervous system, and Virgoans must beware of ulcers and nervous instability.

Libra

Librans, considered the most desirable of zodiacal types by many modern astrologers, are usually good-looking and elegant, their charm, courtesy and optimism mediated to everyone around them by their sometimes mediumistic intuition. Naturally kind, loathing cruelty and with an urge towards unity in human relationships, they use their optimistic natures for the perfectionism they desire in social living. They cooperate and compromise with everyone around them, loving harmony and detesting conflict between people. They are consequently sometimes accused of being colourless, timid, changeable, indecisive and conventional, and it is true that they depend on others to shake them out of their apparent easy-going inertness. Seldom angry, they can explode into shockingly articulate rages and can be impatient of routine.

They are artistic rather than scholarly, with good perception and observation and a critical ability which gives them integrity, a sense of justice and a dislike of extremes. They can resolve conflicts by compromise and meet claims against themselves even to their disadvantage. They are trustworthy in handling other people's money, but may squander their own goods and talents in over-enthusiasm for new causes.

Librans like the opposite sex. In spite of a romanticism bordering on sentimentality, their marriages are often unions of minds, happy because they tolerate the beloved's failings.

They are never vulgar or vicious, but may be frivolous, shallow, flirtatious, profligate, too easy-going and pleasure-loving. Libran men sometimes gamble recklessly and are inclined to promiscuity; women can be careless about money, jealous, impatient of criticism and greedy for approval.

Their talents make them diplomats, civil servants, administrators, lawyers, experts in feminine clothes and cosmetics, social workers, valuers, writers, artists, critics and composers. The men make good speculators, with the optimism and ability to recover from financial crashes. Librans dislike coarse, dirty toil but their work for humanity when self-disciplined can be magnificent. They are sometimes modestly content, sometimes ambitious, and 'lazy Libra' may be surprisingly energetic.

Libra governs the kidneys and lumbar region and Librans are susceptible to kidney complaints and lumbago.

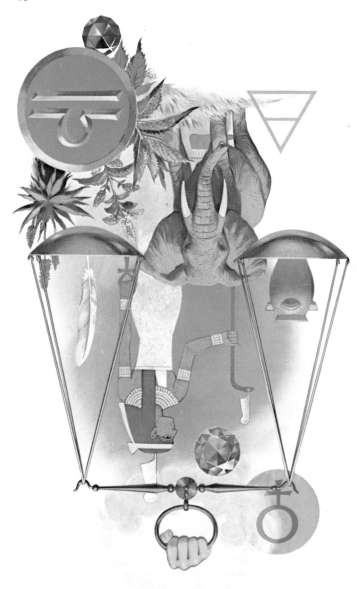

Scorpio

Scorpios are the intensest and profoundest of the zodiacal types. They are power-houses of emotional energy which makes them immensely forceful towards others and subject to extremes of likes or dislikes. They can be utterly unconventional, but can also harness their intensity constructively. In society they are courteous, affable, magnanimous, dignified, reserved and thoughtful in conversation, often possessing penetrating eyes and a magnetic personality. In their work, in which ambition drives them on, they can relate to others only as leaders and can be blunt to the point of cruelty. Their will-power is immense and their depth of character and passionate conviction sometimes overwhelming. They are sensitive, particularly to injury, being jealous of honour, quick to anger and of volatile temperament. Their inner intensity can express itself in the spiritual fervour of the mystic, the detached self-control of the surgeon, the heroism of the soldier.

They have strong reasoning powers combined with imagination, intuition, critical perception and an analytical capacity, and can penetrate skilfully to profundities beyond the average. The most sexually energetic of all the signs, they are capable of great heights of passionate ecstasy but also of using their power sadistically and of becoming monsters of sensuality and eroticism. Their overriding urge is to use their powers to penetrate beyond themselves and to lose themselves sexually in another human being in an almost religious mystical ecstasy, thus discovering the meaning of that humanity which is greater than the individual being.

Their faults are brooding resentment, vindictiveness, roughness, deliberate cruelty, aggressive brutality, arrogance, jealousy, discarding friends when their usefulness is exhausted, intense love of praise and flattery, procrastination and indolence. The intensity of their natures exaggerates harmful tendencies into vices far greater than normal.

Scorpios make the best surgeons and can be soldiers, detectives, lawyers, physicists, psychologists, orators and writers – any profession in which research, analysis, dealing with practicalities, and solving of mysteries are relevant. Their mystical capabilities can make them spiritual healers. The sign rules the genitals, bladder and urinary system.

Sagittarius

Sagittarians need to explore beyond the familiar, geographically and mentally, requiring space and freedom in new lands and dimensions of thought. Their many virtues include idealism, optimism even after frequent disappointments, generosity, sincerity and love of justice. They are versatile, magnanimous, forgiving, modest and honourable, often religious and moral, witty, and respectful towards age.

Intellectually they are deep, wide, tolerant, with foresight and judgement, the ability to initiate and the urge to understand. Their thought is impetuous and intuitive, sometimes original; they are better adapters than inventors.

In love, Sagittarians, though ardent and sincere, are conventional, able to control their sexuality. While uncongenial unions can bring disaster, failure to win the beloved may embitter their whole lives. They are faithful and indulgent to their families, but treat the home as a base from which to sally forth on their travels, sometimes too busy to be loving and needing to feel free. Sagittarian women may find it difficult to express affection.

Their restlessness, intrepid adventurousness and ambition, leading perhaps to ruthless lust for leadership, makes them avoid the monotonous hard slog. Their extreme professionalism and will to power are tempered by pleasant manners. Their various talents suit the church, law, philosophy, politics, the civil service, public relations, social administration and teaching in one direction, travel and exploration in another, music in a third and sporting pursuits with cars, aeroplanes and animals in a fourth. They are good sports coaches though their sporting instinct may lead them into imprudent gambling.

Their possible vices are boisterousness, vulgarity, dangerous fanaticism, extravagance, tactlessness, boasting and inconsiderateness. Angered easily, they flare up over trifles, so bluntly spoken as to hurt needlessly. Impatient, they rush every plan through immediately, expecting too much of others and scornful of their inadequacies, yet demanding recognition of their own efforts. These may be considerable, for they can sacrifice their health and their families to complete a project once they have begun it. Exacting, domineering, they may be

too moralizing and 'sick of self-love', or playboys wasting their lives away. Some are inclined to superstitious fears, neglect of their duties, and hypocrisy disguised by a false joviality.

Sagittarians are susceptible to ailments of the hips, thighs and sciatic nerves which the sign governs.

Capricorn

Capricornians are mankind's stabilizers. They are serious, hardworking, persistent against hardship, boredom or frustration, unemotional, often humourless, sometimes pessimistic and over-cautious, but responsible, just, economical without meanness, clear-headed, independent, and faithful friends who always keep promises. If happy they are ecstatic, if miserable wretched indeed, often without knowing why. They set themselves high standards, carefully planning to fulfil their ambitions, and are honest self-critics. They achieve great results with minimum effort and expense and can do several things simultaneously. They are rock-like characters, tough, determined, practical and resourceful, slow but stubborn, good organizers respecting discipline and authority. They neither meddle with others nor allow interference with themselves.

Their minds are calculating, rational and severe. They think deeply, have excellent memories and are insatiable yet controlled in their desire for knowledge. Concentration and subtlety make them succinct writers, shrewd, pertinent public speakers and in debate, which they love, adepts at luring their opponents into traps and confounding them with logic. Though sceptical, they are interested in the occult. Mathematics and music attract them. They are not original but develop what others initiate, and can be surprisingly witty and subtle for the prosaic creatures they appear to be.

Capricornians are cautious in affection, sometimes even disliking the opposite sex. But they are faithful in marriage though inclined to jealousy. In the past they have been accused of lechery and inconstancy, but not today. Family life has too strong a place in their appreciation of an ordered community.

They can work as economists, scientists, managers, engineers, mathematicians and builders. They make good teachers, especially principals, and can excel as civil servants, politicians and even entertainers. Any work in which practical business ability allied with tact is needed, combined with a hidden drive of ambition added to love of power and wealth, can suit Capricornians.

Their faults may be bigotry, selfishness, severity spilling into cruelty, and pessimism which makes them worry unnecessarily and depresses their colleagues. They can be too

conventional and careless about their personal appearance, and their thrift can degenerate into miserliness.

Knees and skin are Capricorn's domain, and Capricornians may suffer from knee troubles, rashes and digestion upsets caused by worry and the suppression of their emotions.

Aquarius

Several Aquarian types exist. Generally they are quiet, gentle, persevering without self-assertion, speak moderately and reasonably, show strong will and conviction, and are frank, genial, serious, refined and idealistic. They respect neither convention nor authority, seeing through pomp and pretentiousness; though original, progressive thinkers, they are too intelligent and tolerant to be destructive revolutionaries, for all their energetic approval of causes, however extreme, which they support. A philosophical and spiritual bent can drive them into an ivory tower where they reflect on abstract problems irrelevant to life, but may equally inspire them to scientific research which fulfils their philanthropic ideals.

One Aquarian type is patient, shy, sensitive and independent, resenting even helpful interference. Another is lively and exhibitionist. Both may have a dry humour and lack pretentiousness. Both will be intelligent, intuitive (sometimes clairvoyant), imaginative, inventive, concise, clear and logical. Aquarians seek truth above all things, their breadth of vision bringing diverse factors into a whole. They are sufficiently honest to change their opinions, though held with conviction, if evidence convinces them they are wrong.

In spite of their desire to benefit humanity, they make few friends. They do not give themselves easily and are sometimes thought cold. If disillusioned, they do not forgive. But they are good judges of human nature, can exert irresistible mental attraction on those they love, including the opposite sex, will sacrifice everything for them and be faithful for life.

They work best in group projects. Their feeling of oneness with nature and passion for truth make them excellent scientists and they can express their progressiveness as writers, broadcasters, publishers, welfare workers and teachers. They may excel in photography, radiography, electronics, aviation, almost everything technical. They sometimes have healing gifts, and can be good character actors and musicians.

Their faults are fanatical eccentricity, overmuch detachment and lack of integrity, expressed in cunning, secretiveness and broken promises. Rudeness, erratic temper and misanthropy may submerge their virtues. Aquarius governs the legs from knees to ankles and the circulation.

Pisces

Pisceans have a fluid nature, emotional, compassionate, reflecting the feelings of those around them and usually responding with the utmost sympathy to suffering. They dislike discipline and confinement within codes of behaviour.

They are extremely imaginative, instinctive rather than intellectual, versatile, receptive and intuitive. Will-power and reasoning are weak, and, rather than logic, their faith is in the unknown beyond sense and the material. They tend to live in a dream-world where their mediumistic faculties (susceptible to good or bad psychic influences) can operate, resulting sometimes in unexpectedly remarkable creativity. They love luxury, novel sensations, beauty in nature and art, pleasure and travel in remote exotic places.

They are full of gentle, generous qualities, popular with all kinds of people, reacting to their influence and to the situations in which they find themselves rather than create, and letting problems solve themselves rather than trying to solve them. Their easy-going, loving, honest, submissive natures are often too trusting in marriage, and coarsely sexual partners will make them unhappy, for their natures require a purer, completer relationship. Never egotistical, they give more than they ask, intensely loyal and home-loving, though often disliking household chores.

Pisceans are devoted workers in many fields. Their psychic qualities can make them mystics, priests and mediums. Their ability to imitate and enter the feelings of others may make them actors, writers, artists, critics and even detectives (imagining themselves in the place of the criminal). Their sympathy enables them to care for the sick, needy or animals and their fondness for the remote can turn them into sailors, travellers or astronomers. Many musicians, lawyers and architects are found under this sign, together with workers with fluids, gases, anaesthetics and plastics.

Their faults, exasperating rather than vicious, are unreliability, ruthlessness, gossip, diffidence, indolence, fickleness, gullibility and emotionalism. They can be extremely careless and impractical, indiscreet, intellectually and actually dishonest, indecisive in important matters, yet upholding absurdities with the obstinacy of the weak. Extravagantly temperamental and dependent on others, they can turn to drink and drugs to escape imagined fears, loneliness or in sheer self-indulgence.

Pisces governs the feet, and Pisceans are liable to foot-disorders.

CASTING AND INTERPRETING A HOROSCOPE

In a book of this length only a rule-of-thumb introduction to the casting and interpretation of a horoscope can be given. Casting is simpler than is usually thought; but the inter-relationship of the many factors involved in interpretation may make it complicated indeed and astrologers can disagree over it widely. It is here that psychic intuition is needed rather than rules which at best serve as guide-lines.

All horoscopes, whether of birth, marriage, a ship-launching or the start of a business are calculated in the same way. The student will need paper on which to draw his chart; rough paper for calculations; an Ephemeris for the relevant year (*Raphael's Epheremides*, published for every year from about 1820 is a standard work); a *Pluto Ephemeris* for years before 1930, when the planet was discovered; a *Table of Houses* (*Raphael's Tables of Houses* for Great Britain and northern latitudes are standard); a gazetteer for finding the latitudes and longitudes of places; a list of standard and zone times throughout the world; a table for converting degrees and minutes of longitude into their equivalent in time; and proportional logarithm tables for finding the planets' positions. The reasons for this formidable list will be seen as we work through the steps to be taken.

24		DECEMBER, 1926.								[RAPHAEL'S
D M	**Neptune.**		**Herschel.**		**Saturn.**		**Jupiter.**		**Mars.**	
	Lat.	Dec.	Lat.	Dec.	Lat.	Dec.	Lat.	Dec.	Lat.	Declin.
	° ′	° ′	° ′	° ′	° ′	° ′	° ′	° ′	° ′	° ′ · ° ′
1	0N26	12N56	0S46	2S29	1N50	18S20	0S59	15 S27	0N37	13N42 · 13N42
3	0 26	12 56	0 46	2 29	1 50	18 23	0 59	15 21	0 42	13 43 · 13 45
5	0 26	12 56	0 46	2 29	1 50	18 26	0 59	15 15	0 47	13 46 · 13 48
7	0 26	12 56	0 45	2 28	1 50	18 29	0 59	15 9	0 51	13 50 · 13 52
9	0 26	12 57	0 45	2 28	1 50	18 31	0 59	15 3	0 55	13 54 · 13 57
11	0 27	12 57	0 45	2 28	1 50	18 34	0 59	14 56	0 58	14 0 · 14 3
13	0 27	12 57	0 45	2 27	1 50	18 37	0 58	14 49	1 2	14 6 · 14 9
15	0 27	12 57	0 45	2 27	1 50	18 40	0 58	14 42	1 5	14 13 · 14 16
17	0 27	12 58	0 45	2 26	1 50	18 42	0 58	14 35	1 8	14 20 · 14 25
19	0 27	12 58	0 45	2 26	1 50	18 45	0 58	14 28	1 11	14 29 · 14 33
21	0 27	12 58	0 45	2 25	1 50	18 48	0 58	14 21	1 14	14 38 · 14 43
23	0 27	12 59	0 45	2 25	1 50	18 50	0 58	14 13	1 17	14 48 · 14 53
25	0 27	12 59	0 45	2 24	1 51	18 53	0 57	14 5	1 19	14 58 · 15 3
27	0 27	13 0	0 45	2 23	1 51	18 55	0 57	13 57	1 21	15 9 · 15 15
29	0 27	13 1	0 44	2 22	1 51	18 57	0 57	13 49	1 23	15 20 · 15 26
31	0 27	13 2	0 44	2 21	1 51	19 0	0 57	13 41	1 25	15 32 ·

The exact moment of birth (the cutting of the umbilical cord when the baby begins its separate life) must be known for an accurate horoscope. In practice, this is seldom known accurately, so practitioners allow variations of up to 10° in calculating planetary aspects. The moon takes almost a day to pass through this arc and the other planets move so slowly that they scarcely affect the horoscope's accuracy.

But the turning world moves through the twelve zodiacal signs in twenty-four hours, and sixty minutes' error could result in an entirely inaccurate chart. If the planets are so placed that an error of a few minutes in the time of birth would put them in different signs and houses (see below) a second calculation is often made. Either by working backwards from important events in a man's life (his marriage, a severe illness) – a process known as 'rectification' – or by seeing which of the two calculations fit his outstanding characteristics, the interpreter can tell which is correct. If the time of birth is completely unknown, a 'flat' chart is drawn with Aries 0° on the cusp of the first house and the planets placed in their noon positions on the birthday. But this is too approximate to be satisfactory.

Tables from *Raphael's Astrological Ephemeris* for 1926

EPHEMERIS.] **DECEMBER, 1926.** 25

D M	Venus. Lat.	Venus. Declin.	Venus. Declin.	Mercury. Lat.	Mercury. Declin.	Mercury. Declin.	☽ Node.
	° ′	° ′	° ′	° ′	° ′	° ′	° ′
1	0N 3	22S 3	22S16	2N17	17S11	16S53	8♋36
3	0S 2	22 28	22 39	2 33	16 40	16 32	8 29
5	0 7	22 50	23 0	2 41	16 28	16 28	8 23
7	0 12	23 9	23 17	2 42	16 32	16 39	8 17
9	0 17	23 25	23 32	2 38	16 49	17 1	8 10
11	0 21	23 39	23 44	2 30	17 16	17 32	8 4
13	0 26	23 49	23 54	2 19	17 49	18 8	7 57
15	0 31	23 57	24 0	2 6	18 28	18 48	7 51
17	0 35	24 2	24 3	1 51	19 8	19 29	7 45
19	0 39	24 3	24 3	1 36	19 49	20 9	7 38
21	0 44	24 3	24 0	1 21	20 29	20 49	7 32
23	0 48	23 58	23 55	1 5	21 8	21 27	7 26
25	0 52	23 51	23 46	0 49	21 45	22 2	7 19
27	0 56	23 40	23 34	0 33	22 18	22 33	7 13
29	1 0	23 27	23 20	0 17	22 48	23 1	7 7
31	1 3	23 11		0 2	23 14		7 0

Mutual Aspects.

1. ♀ ± ♂. ☿ □ ♅.
2. ☉ Q ♃.
3. ☉ ± ♂. ☿ △ ♅.
7. ☿ △ ♅.
8. ♀ ⚼ ♂.
10. ♀ ✶ ♃. ☿ □ ♆.
12. ☉ ⚼ ♆. ♂ Q ♃.
13. ♀ □ ♅.
14. ♀ △ ♆.
15. ☿ ☌ ♄.
16. ☉ ✶ ♃. ☿ P ♄.
17. ♀ ⚻ ♄.
18. ☉ □ ♅. ☿ ▽ ♂.
19. ☉ △ ♆. ♂ P ♃.
21. ♀ △ ♂.
23. ☿ ± ♂. ♀ ⊥ ♄.
24. ♀ ∠ ♃. ☿ Q ♃.
25. ☉ ⚻ ♄. ♀ ⚼ ♆.
27. ♀ Q ♅.
29. ♃ ⚻ ♅.
30. ☉ △ ♂.
31. ☉ ⊥ ♄, P ☿. ☿ ⚼ ♂, P ♀. ♀ ∠ ♄.

If the time of birth is known in local time, British Summer Time or Double Summer Time, it must be translated into Greenwich Mean Time (the Ephemerides give the dates of B.S.T. and D.S.T. respectively), then into sidereal time. This is time measured by the apparent diurnal motion of the stars, the sidereal day being just under four minutes shorter than the solar day. The steps to be taken, numbered for the sake of simplicity, are:

1. Let us use as a working example an oft-quoted horoscope of a personality whom we shall call X, born at 9.09 a.m. local time at Los Angeles, USA, on 1 June 1926. The list of zone times shows that to convert this to Greenwich Mean Time eight hours must be added, giving 5.09 p.m. Our starting point for sidereal time is noon on 1 January 1926 (for a birth before midday we should choose midnight on 1 January) for which the ephemeris gives 18 hours, 42 minutes.

2. Add to this hours and minutes for each month according to the following table, the top figure for a common year, the bottom for a leap year:

Feb.		March		April		May		June		July	
h.	m.	h.	m.	h.	m.	h.	m.	h.	m.	h.	m.
2	2	3	52	5	55	7	53	9	55	11	54
2	2	3	56	5	59	7	57	9	59	11	58

Aug.		Sept.		Oct.		Nov.		Dec.	
h.	m.	h.	m.	h.	m.	h.	m.	h.	m.
13	56	15	58	17	56	19	59	21	57
14	00	16	02	18	00	20	02	22	01

18 hours, 42 minutes+9 hours, 55 minutes = 28 hours, 37 minutes.

3. Next, add hours and minutes for days:

2nd	4m.	8th	28m.	14th	51m.	20th	1h. 15m.	26th	1h. 39m.
3rd	8m.	9th	32m.	15th	55m.	21st	1h. 19m.	27th	1h. 42m.
4th	12m.	10th	35m.	16th	59m.	22nd	1h. 23m.	28th	1h. 46m.
5th	16m.	11th	39m.	17th	63m.	23rd	1h. 27m.	29th	1h. 50m.
6th	20m.	12th	43m.	18th	67m.	24th	1h. 31m.	30th	1h. 54m.
7th	24m.	13th	47m.	19th	71m.	25th	1h. 35m.	31st	1h. 58m.

As X was born on 1 June, nothing is added.

4. For each degree of westward longitude subtract four minutes; for each degree of eastward longitude add four. The latitude and longitude of Los Angeles are 34° N, 118° W. 118 × 4m = 7 hours, 52 minutes. 28 hours, 37 minutes − 7 hours, 52 minutes = 20 hours, 45 minutes (sidereal time on 1 June).

5. Add the time of birth (called the interval) already corrected to G.M.T. 20 hours, 45 minutes+5 hours, 9 minutes = 25 hours, 54 minutes.

6. Add one minute for births occurring three to nine hours after midnight or midday, two for ten to twelve hours (nothing for one to two hours). This gives us here 25 hours, 55 minutes.

7. If the total exceeds 24 hours we subtract 24, giving us 1 hour, 55 minutes. For births in the southern hemisphere add twelve hours to the local sidereal time for a birth at the same latitude north. The ascendant and M.C. are placed in the signs opposite those in a northern hemisphere horoscope; here, for example (see diagram, p. 93), the ascendant would be in

The meanings of the 1st, 2nd and 3rd houses, illustrated

Aquarius and the M.C. in Scorpio. The signs in which the planets are placed, however, are not reversed.

8. We now come to the houses, sometimes called 'mundane' because they concern earthly activities, represented in the diagram (p. 93) by 30° segments ('lunes') divided by 'spokes' ('cusps'). The houses are numbered 1–12 anticlockwise, the cusp of the first house always coinciding with the ascendant placed at 9 o'clock on the chart. The meanings of the houses are:

First: Childhood, beginning, individuality, the subject's character, appearance, general tendencies, self-centred interests and inclinations to particular illnesses. Sign, Aries; planet, Mars.

Second: Possessions, income, expenditure, personal security, comfort and contentment, the native's personal uniqueness, capabilities and resourcefulness. Sign, Taurus; planet, Venus.

Third: Short journeys, communication and direct mental contact with others in conversation and letters, the subject's relationship with his environment, especially family and

The meanings of the 4th, 5th and 6th houses, illustrated

84

The meanings of the 7th, 8th and 9th houses, illustrated

neighbours. Sign, Gemini; planet, Mercury.

Fourth: Birthplace, home, buildings, property owned and rented, parents, close relatives, as the base from which the native develops his own life, closing years of life. Sign, Cancer; planet, the moon.

Fifth: Re-creation in the narrow and wide senses of amusement, entertainment, sport, pleasure, happiness, gambling, creativeness, practically and artistically, the organizing of personal tastes and qualities into a projection of the native's image, sex, love-affairs, children and brain-children (ideas). Sign, Leo; planet, the sun.

Sixth: Physical conditions, work, food, health, all the factors making for a life-pattern enabling the native to serve his community and receive his due of service from his employees. Sign, Virgo; planet, Mercury.

Seventh: Identification of the self with others at the personal levels of marriage, business partnerships, etc., with the opposite in war and legal conflict. The seventh house can suggest the type of marriage partner suited to the native's personality. Sign, Libra; planet, Mercury.

Eighth: Loss and death, including perhaps the kind of death threatened, matters to do with wills and legacies, material dependence on others, self-sacrifice, resources shared with others, death to former ways in conversion to new ideas. Sign, Scorpio; planet, Mars.

Ninth: Distant horizons, far adventuring in both a physical and spiritual sense, higher education, research, religion, philosophy, the ferment and communication of ideas, the subject's church or other faith as an organization, relatives not of his blood (in-laws), relationships with foreigners. Sign, Sagittarius; planet, Jupiter.

Tenth: Interests outside the home; the native's establishment in his career, his social status, public position and responsibilities in the community, the achievement or disappointment of his ambitions, fame or notoriety. Sign, Capricorn; planet, Saturn.

Eleventh: Group relationships, as distinct from personal aims and ambitions, creative activities in societies and organizations, friendships in such groups, reformative activities, possibly unconventional. Sign, Aquarius; planet, Saturn *or* Uranus.

The meanings of the 10th, 11th and 12th houses, illustrated

Twelfth: Activities and factors limiting the ability to experience life wholly – personal limitations, social barriers, imprisonment, monastic life, hospitals, mental institutions, heavy sorrow, self-denying activities, self-imposed limitations in escapist day-dreaming, withdrawal from reality, self disintegration and a secret inner life or involvement in secret activities, societies and conspiracies. Sign, Pisces; planet, Jupiter *or* Neptune.

Any planet or sign placed in its corresponding house reinforces the relationship; the life-principle represented by the planet functions in the typical way represented by the sign focussing on the activities represented by the house.

9. We must next find the ascendant, which is the point of the ecliptic, and the sign of the zodiac rising above the horizon at the moment of birth. Looking up latitude 34° N in the Table of Houses, we find figures given not for 1 hour, 55 minutes but for 1.48 and 2.0 as follows:

1h 48m M.C. 29 ♈ 3   Ascendant 7 ♌ 33
2h 00m M.C. 2 ♉ 11   Ascendant 10 ♌ 1

The difference between the two M.C.s is 3° 8 minutes, or 188 minutes. This sum divided by twelve (2 hours, 0 minutes minus 1 hour, 48 minutes) multiplied by seven (1 hour, 55 minutes minus 1 hour, 48 minutes) gives 1° 50 minutes, to be added to 29 ♈ 3, giving, to the nearest degree, an M.C. 1° ♉ and an ascendant of 9° ♌ The novice need not be concerned with the formulae that exist for the exact calculation of the ascendant and M.C.

Since the ascendant coincides with the cusp of the twelfth and first houses, the cusp of every house will be at 9° of a zodiac sign (see diagram, p. 93). We can also insert the M.C. at 1° ♉.

10. Next, we must insert the planets in their positions calculated from the Ephemeris. At noon on 1 June 1926, the sun was 10° 13′ in Gemini, written as 10 ♊ 13; Mercury at 6° ♊ 18; Venus at 28 ♈ 30; Mars at 20 ♓ 35; Jupiter at 26 ♒ 49; Saturn at 21 ♏ 27 R (R means that a planet is retrograde, apparently moving back along its track, owing to the angle of the earth and the planets in their orbits); Uranus at 29 ♓ 0; Neptune at 22 ♌ 13; Pluto at 13 ♋ 24, and the moon at 15 ♒ 50. The only planets which move significantly are the moon, covering about 3° in five hours and Mercury, about $\frac{1}{2}$°.

Venus moves a little less, other planets scarcely at all. We can therefore round off all the planetary positions to the nearest degree, plotting the moon as 19˘ ♒ and Mercury as 7 ♊.

Later, the student will want to calculate planetary positions more exactly. If his subject was born after midday he works from the noon of the birthday; if before, from the noon of the previous day. In the Ephemeris the column headed '☉ Long.' gives the sun's longitudinal positions on successive days. Let us call these 'a' and 'b'; a minus b gives c, the number of minutes travelled by the sun in 24 hours.

The table of proportional logarithms has horizontal columns numbered 0 to 15 degrees or hours, and a left-hand vertical column of minutes numbered 0 to 59. We first find the log of the interval (in our example 5 hours, 9 minutes) by travelling down the column 5 of degrees and hours till we reach the horizontal marking 9 minutes. We similarly find the log for the sun's daily movement of 'd' minutes, adding the two together to give a figure 'e'. We search the table of logs. for the figure nearest 'e' and translate it into minutes. If the birth is after noon we add this to the sun's longitudinal position at noon; if before noon, we subtract it. The process may be repeated for the moon, Mercury, Venus and Mars, but the positions of Jupiter, Saturn, Uranus, Neptune and Pluto may be calculated by simple proportion.

11. The planet aspects must now be measured, for these are important for the horoscope's interpretation. Aspects are measured between two planets or a planet and the ascendant or M.C. along the ecliptic in degrees and minutes of celestial longitude. An allowance either side of an aspect of so many degrees (called an orb) is allowed by astrologers who regard planets 'within orb' as aspected. Aspects between planets accentuate the characteristics associated with them, producing strong or weak psychological tendencies which the native must use or guard against.

There are ten aspects:

(Opposite) The relative positions of the planets in various aspects and the aspect signs

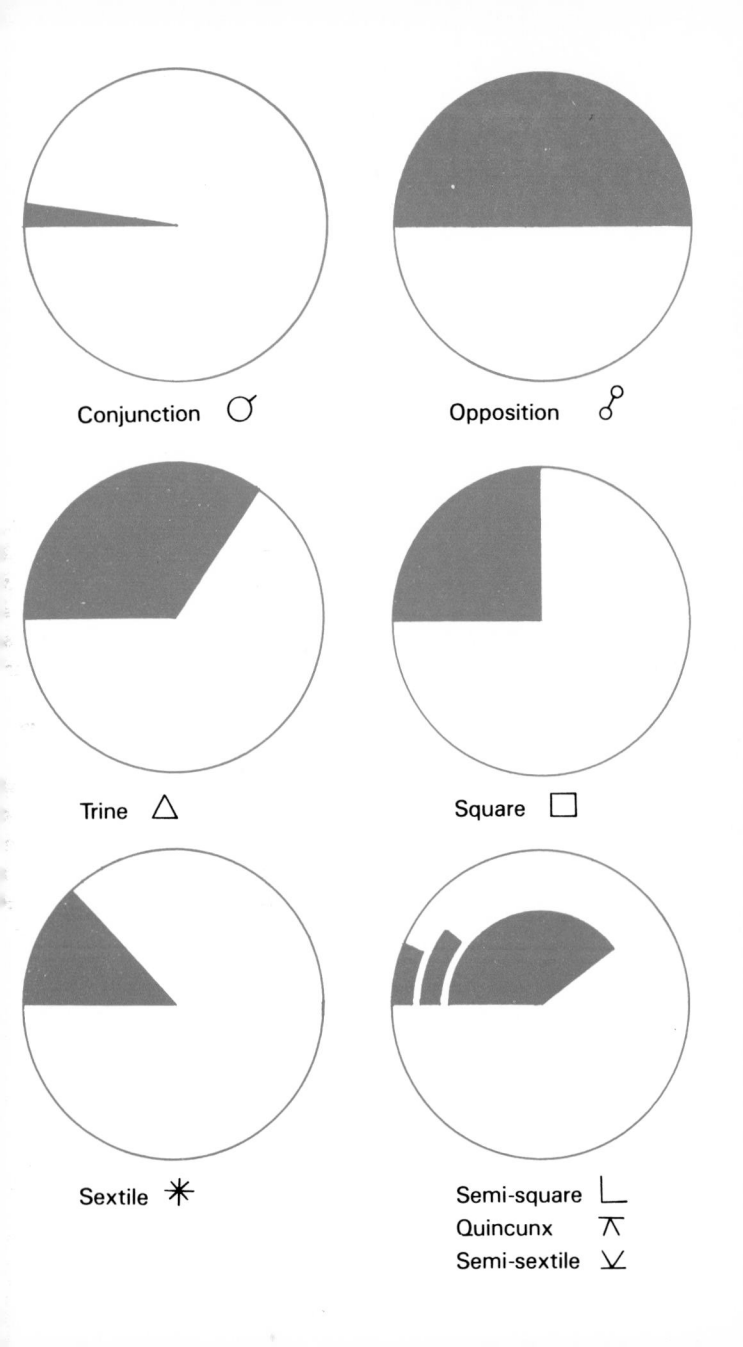

Conjunction ♂

Opposition ⁂

Trine △

Square □

Sextile ✱

Semi-square ∟
Quincunx ⊼
Semi-sextile ⊻

Aspect	Name	Orb	Symbol	Zodiacal signs apart (approx.)	Force
0°	conjunction	8°	☌	0	strong
30°	semi-sextile	2°	⊻	1	weak
45°	semi-square	2°	∟	2	weak
60°	sextile	6°	✳	2	moderate
90°	square	8°	□	3	strong
120°	trine	8°	△	4	strong
135°	sesquiquadrate	2°	⊡	5	weak
150°	quincunx	2°	⊼	5-6	weak
180°	opposition	8°	☍	6	strong
0°	parallel of declination	1½°	P	—	strong

Conjunction: The planets' principles will combine in powerful unity with each other. Mars in conjunction with Jupiter is written ♂ ☌ ♃ and the other aspects are similarly expressed.

Semi-sextile, semi-square, sesquiquadrate, quincunx: Although of minor importance, indicate conditions requiring a conscious effort by the subject to use or overcome.

Sextile: Indicates a moderate harmonious influence of the good characteristics if the planets and signs concerned are given equal attention.

Square: Is a discordant influence which can cause frustration, imbalance and inner conflict. But it can be turned into a source of strength and success by a character strong enough to use the untethered energies to overcome difficulties which will crush a weak personality.

Trine: Brings a harmonious influence similar to but more powerful than the sextile's. The danger here is that prosperity or success coming too easily may further enfeeble an already weak character.

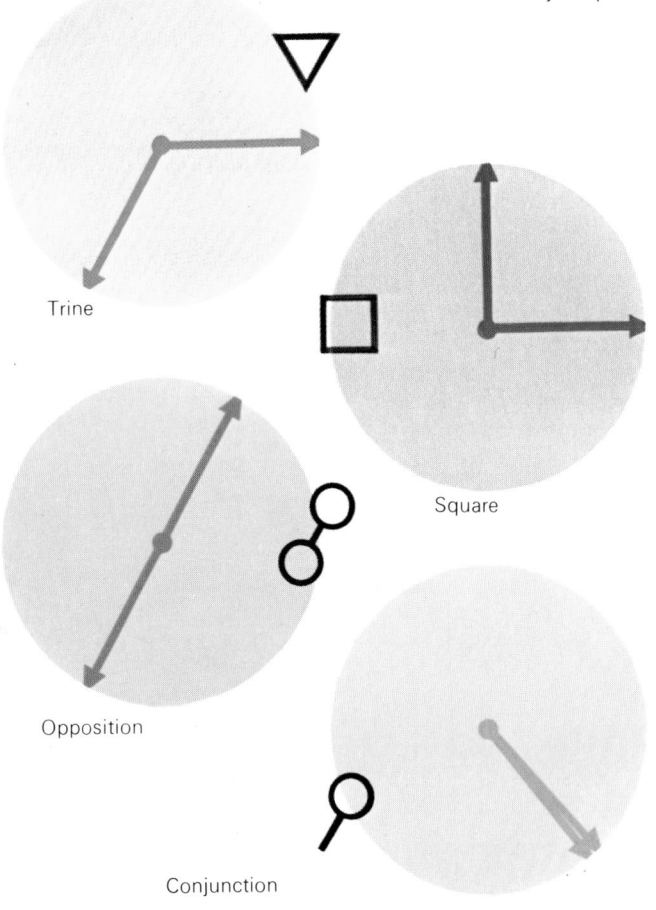

The four major aspects

Trine

Square

Opposition

Conjunction

Opposition: Indicates tension, even hostility, between the planets and signs involved, resulting in a possible Jekyll and Hyde inner conflict of character. Again, a negative result is not inevitable. By developing equally the positive complimentary characteristics of the opposing elements the native can resolve the conflict and evolve a wholeness of character which includes them all.

Parallel: The declination of a planet corresponds with terrestrial latitude and is measured in degrees and minutes north and south of the equator. Planets with the same declinations are 'parallel', reinforcing each other if on the same side of the equator, in opposition if on opposite sides. The declination of all the planets except the moon can be calculated proportionately. If the moon is increasing in declination its motion must be added, if decreasing it must be subtracted, according to the following scheme:

Moon's declination, 31 May 1926	....
Moon's declination, 1 June 1926	....
	— —
Moon's motion of declination	....
Log. of motion of declination	....
Log. of motion of declination	....
Log. of interval (5 hours, 9 minutes)	....
	— —
Addition of logs.	....
Nearest figure to this addition	....
Moon's declination 1 June	....
Moon's declination during interval	....
	— —
Moon's declination at birth	....

12. Approximately every 27 days the moon completes a nodical revolution, its path apparently crossing the ecliptic from south to north (the ascending or north node ☊) and from north to south (the descending or south node ☋). The position of the north node relative to sign, house and aspects is thought to indicate benefits received through no effort of the native (for example, an unexpected legacy). That of the south node indicates ill-health in the part of the body associated with the sign in which the node is found, or something which will handicap the native, demanding from him unrewarded sacrifice. The north node is shown in the Ephemeris, the south occupying the opposite point in the ecliptic. The north node on 1 June, 1926 was 18° ♋ 17', the south 18° ♑ 17'.

The complete interpretation of a horoscope may take some days because of the many factors to be studied, the influences of which have to be balanced against each other. Even the most straightforward lives and characters are open to trends and possibilities which may or may not be realized, and it is these that a horoscope shows, not sure predictions of future events as is sometimes popularly thought.

The novice interpreter must first work fairly mechanically, mastering the vocabulary and grammar of astrology. Next, he must adopt a system by which he studies a chart so as not to omit important factors. Thirdly, he must try to develop that insight which will enable him to understand a chart intuitively. A very few may have genius in this. Others will develop intuitive interpretation according to their abilities and enthusiasm. The process is not unlike writing or painting: a writer learns vocabulary and grammar, a painter composition, design and the techniques of using his media, and they can become adequate in words or on canvas by practice and application. A very few will become literary giants or great masters. It is the same with astrology.

The following outline of a method of interpretation is no

X's horoscope

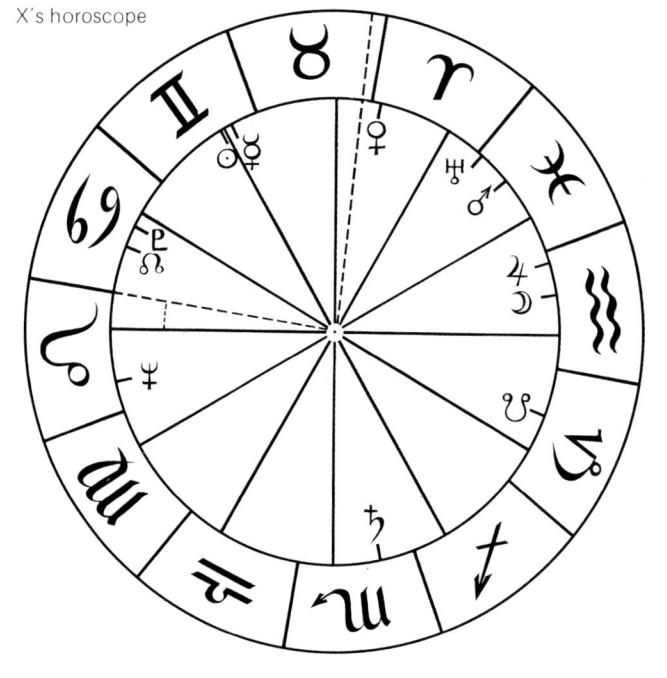

more than a guide. Every student must develop his own method, making sure that he omits no vital factor. The first step is to note the meaning of each factor. Some of these meanings will appear inconsistent with or even contradict each other. The second step is to work out the comparative strengths of the contradictions so that the native may learn what characteristics in himself he must nurture by discipline and learning and the weaknesses and inconsistencies he must guard against and eradicate. The third step is to write a complete interpretation including all the information gleaned from the many elements present in the chart. The method detailed here is only one among many.

1. General features from (a) the lunar nodes; (b) the positive and negative classifications of the planets (excluding Neptune, Uranus and Pluto), the ascendant and M.C. from the signs in which they are placed; (c) the triplicities; (d) the quadruplicities; (e) main aspect patterns.

2. The ascendant sign.

3. The ascendant ruler in its sign position and house.

4. The sun in its sign and house (if Leo is in the ascendant, this will be the same as 3).

5. The moon in its sign and house (if Cancer is the ascendant sign, this will be the same as 3).

Table of aspects

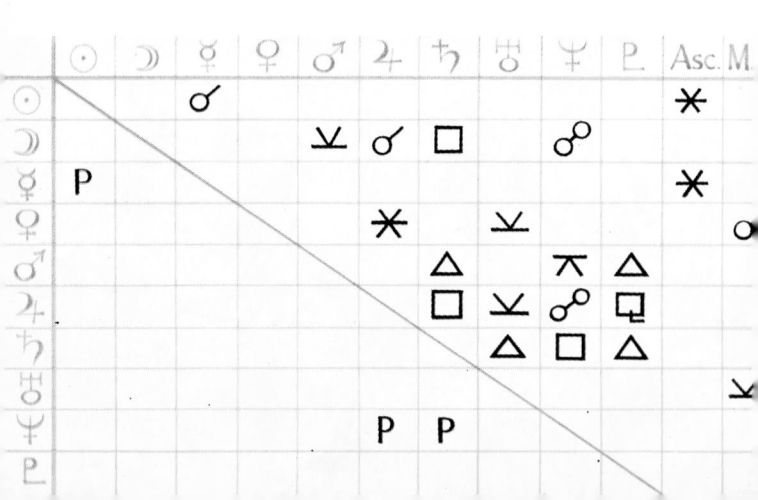

6. Angular planets (i.e. those within an 8° orb of conjunction with the ascendant, M.C., descendant and I.C.).

7. The individual planets.

8. The aspects.

Following these steps in X's chart we have:

1a. ◯ in twelfth and seventh houses.

b. Six of the planets, ascendant and M.C. are in positive signs, three in negative.

c. Triplicities: four air, four water, two fire, no earth; excluding Neptune, Uranus and Pluto, which influence generations rather than individuals, four air, two water, one fire.

d. Quadruplicities: four fixed, four mutable, two cardinal; or, again excluding the outer planets, three fixed, three mutable, one cardinal.

e. Main aspect patterns: one Grand Trine of three planets, Pluto, Mars and Saturn, in trine with each other; two T-squares of two planets in opposition, each square to a third – Neptune opposed to Jupiter are both square to Saturn, and the moon and Neptune in opposition are square to Saturn.

2. Ascendant sign: Leo.

3. Ascendant ruler in sign and house. The sun in Gemini and the eleventh house.

4. As 3.

5. The moon is in Aquarius and the seventh house.

6. There is one angular planet in the chart, Venus in Aries and the ninth house, 3° from the M.C.

7. The individual planets in their signs and houses.

8. The aspects. In the table opposite the minor as well as the major aspects are given for completeness' sake. The compilation of such a table ensures that no aspect is missed. Only the major aspects will be interpreted here. N indicates 'None'.

We next note the meanings of each feature of the chart.

1a. The lunar nodes indicate benefits which come, strangely, from the subject's self-limitations. They could proceed from self-discipline or from strength gained through facing frustration, difficulty or sorrow, or from X's secret inner life, private activities or the escapist day-dreaming indicated by other factors in the horoscope. On the other hand, marriage, business partnerships and personal relationships may harm X, imposing effort and sacrifice likely to prove too great and to go unrewarded.

1b. suggests a nature more self-expressive, active and spontaneous than repressed, passive and disciplined.

1c. indicates a character communicative in an emotional way, mentally active, intuitive, with reasonable energy and assertiveness but a marked lack of the practical down-to-earth discipline needed to balance its emotionalism and fantasy-mongering.

1d. shows intenseness and steadiness, counter-balanced by changeableness which, although helped by the subject's adaptability, could make for fickleness and lack of 'sticka-bility'. The character is reasonably enterprising.

1e. The Grand Trine pattern can be beneficent in producing an integrated character but bad in that too easy wealth or success may weaken the subject. Here benefit comes from successful self-expression, controlled energy and a disciplined rejection of emotional factors making for inner conflict. The T-square patterns are very gloomy, reinforcing each other in the same direction. They express an inability to accept limitation and self-discipline, leading to intense emotional frustration, disappointment and misunderstandings. Deep depression, acute neurosis, longing to escape life's realities, a desperate search for compensation in sensation-seeking, instability and even disintegration of character can result.

2. The ascendant sign, Leo, indicates a person of striking appearance, blond and blue-eyed rather than dark, self-expressive, energetic, intense, generous and creative.

3. The ascendant ruler in sign and house, the sun in Gemini and the eleventh house, reveal a dual nature, clever, versatile, happy, charming, elusive, adaptable, and communicative on the one hand, but nervous, restlessly excitable, inconstant and superficial on the other. This nature can love ardently but criticize the beloved fiercely, an uncertain recipe for successful marriage. The eleventh house is concerned with the self's identification with group-objectives, so X will find fulfilment in activity needing the involvement of a number of people. The sun's rulership of Leo intensifies these factors.

4. As 3.

5. The moon in Aquarius shows an imaginative and intense

The relationship of planets to zodiac in the selected horoscope

but dispassionate, detached, open, naive, courteous personality which can be aloof, withdrawn, nervy, unpredictable and erratic. A combination of tastes for things artistic and intellectual makes for marked ability in acting and entertainment. The seventh house, concerned with the identification of the self with others on a personal level, especially in partnerships and marriage, with the moon's influence for changes of habit and residence, gives little hope for permanent relationships.

6. Venus in Aries reveals strong feeling, affection, ardent love and popularity. The negative side of the combination is egotism and, possibly, sensuality. The ninth house concerns far horizons either literally in travel or mentally in experience

beyond the commonplace, to be found in mysticism or at least in day-dreaming and fantasizing. There could be suggested here a character popular with colleagues but dreaming of an impossible romantic love, with a creativeness expressed in showmanship, an Aries feature.

7. Mercury, Mars, Jupiter and Saturn remain (the novice should ignore Uranus, Neptune and Pluto).

Mercury in Gemini accentuates self-expression, communication with others, adaptability and spontaneity. There are also the restlessness and liking for variety and change to be found elsewhere in the chart, together with fickleness and inconsistency. These characteristics are here associated with self-expression outside the home in community life and career and make for success in some form of communication.

Mars in Pisces and the eighth house suggest generosity, arising from intense warmth of feeling, in sharing possessions with others. There may, however, be instability, shown in an extreme blowing of hot and cold.

Jupiter in Aquarius reveals tolerant, humane characteristics if beneficent, tendencies to the opposite and to impatience and tactlessness if badly aspected. The seventh house being that of personal relationships, their success seems unlikely, for of the three main aspects of Jupiter here, two are bad and the good one is the weakest.

Saturn in Scorpio and the fourth house allies a strong sense of purpose with a holding back of self in the inner life that may spill over into selfishness, moodiness and suspicion of the motives of others. The fourth house is concerned with the home and Saturn's relationships and position in the chart strongly suggest an unhappy childhood.

8. The Aspects; a. ☉ ☍ ☿ This aspect shows a good mind and ability in self-expression but can also indicate nervous instability and morbid desire for change.

b. ☉ ⚹ Ascendant. Indicates a personality able to face life and work confidently if at peace with itself.

c. ☉ P ☿ Since both planets share a northern declination, their association is favourable, confirming the trends of the conjunction of the sun and Mercury. (see 8a.)

d. ☽ ☌ ♃ Underlines a quality appearing elsewhere in the chart, that sympathetic and social side of X's character

capable of generous response to the warmth of others.

e. ☽ □ ♄ Suggests deeply depressed moods inspired by the emotional disappointments of an over-sensitive character expecting more from others than they are able to give.

f. ☽ ☍ ♆ Emphasizes the emotional instability and escapist tendencies seen elsewhere in the horoscope, with possible mental confusion and chaos to the point of neurosis.

g. ☿ ⚹ Ascendant. See 7 above.

h. ☿ ⚹ ♃ More successful self-expression, possibly helped by the subject's good looks, Venus being the planet of beauty.

i. ♀ ☌ M.C. Friendly, artistic.

j. ♂ △ ♃ Another factor illustrating self-expression, in art or business.

k. ♂ △ ♇ Makes for constructive control of energies within the personality.

l. ♃ □ ♄ Suggests grievous handicaps through an inability to use the character's positive qualities to fight the negative.

m. ♃ ☍ ♆ Emphasizes the escapist and chaotic characteristics.

n. ♃ △ M.C. Accentuates the traits of Sagittarius, the sign associated with Jupiter – the need for freedom, in love and other departments of life, restlessness and versatility.

o. ♃ ♇ ♆ Jupiter's southern declination and Neptune's northern increase the strength of their opposition (see 8m).

p. ♄ △ ♅ Yet another factor in the chart making for self-expression.

q. ♄ □ ♆ Again a suggestion of emotional upsets leading to neurosis.

r. ♄ △ ♇ A remedial influence giving some control of conflicting forces within the personality.

s. ♄ ♇ ♆ Another opposition, confirming the negative features accentuated in 8q.

Although Uranus is not considered individually in its sign and house, its accompanying Mars in the eighth house suggests sudden unnatural death. This is confirmed by the prominence of Neptune which puts the subject at risk from suffering a mysterious death and from accidents or drugs.

An account of X's character and career deduced from the above data could read as follows:

A physically attractive person who, in spite of an unhappy childhood, grows up to be outwardly happy and extrovert, mentally active and intuitive, with strong generous emotions, spontaneity and versatility. X will be creative and artistic with very great self-expressive and communicative ability, especially in group activity (indicating acting or music rather than literature or art). But the sunny disposition hides a lack of practical application and self-discipline, necessary in an erratic character which the emotionally starved childhood has scarred. Instability, restlessness, superficiality, morbid yearning for change resulting in fickleness, make the success of intimate personal relationships, especially marriage, extremely doubtful. Emotional frustration resulting from the inability to relate may accentuate the character's acute neurosis and depression and impel towards the escapism which is likewise a marked feature – that retreat from life in day-dreams which, in extreme cases, can result in the complete disassociation of insanity or even in self-destruction. The life looks as if it will end in mysterious circumstances.

The horoscope is that of Marilyn Monroe who spent her childhood in eleven foster-homes yet developed into a beautiful, talented and famous film-star with an outwardly gay, attractive, naive and extrovert character. But she suffered from severe depressions and was reported to have made at least four attempts at suicide, while her three unsuccessful marriages show how difficult she found it to relate intimately with others. Her death from barbiturates may have been an accidental overdose taken for the insomnia from which she suffered, it may have been suicide. Neptune, the planet of mystery, guards this secret among its many others.

It is easy to be wise after an event, and a critic of astrology can rightly say that by accentuating different elements in the chart the interpreter could arrive at different conclusions about the subject's character-tendencies and destiny. It remains for our final chapter to try to give the case for and against this mystical science of the stars.

IS ASTROLOGY TRUE?
Changing attitudes

Astrology has existed for thousands of years. But theories about how the planets influence the earth, if they do, have changed from era to era. This is one ground for criticism of astrology: how can a belief be true that is not developing but constantly changing its basis?

The Chaldeans believed that the stars were gods or the habitations of gods who influenced human affairs. The more philosophical Greeks were probably not quite so literal-minded, even though their gods were supposed to dwell on the top of Mount Olympus (did no one ever climb it to find out?). They merely associated the planets with the gods rather than regarding them as gods themselves, though they had many pretty tales of heroes and heroines being turned into constellations after meeting tribulations upon earth.

Sir Isaac Newton, mathematician and astronomer (1642–1727)

Nebula in Cygnus (the swan, in which form Zeus seduced Leda)

Christianity could tolerate none of these ideas, for there was but one God and He supreme. Moreover, free will, which the predestining stars threatened, could not be denied to men. As early as the third century AD Plotinus denied that the stars could cause events. They were signs which announced them, but men could heed their warnings and by the exercise of their free wills in repentance and the submission to the guidance of God could mould their own destinies and avert threatened disaster. Very early, humans had seen that the moon affected the tides and deduced that it and other heavenly bodies might affect them in a similar way. Emanations were sent out which brought astral influences to bear.

Later, a more philosophical type of explanation became popular; there was a harmony throughout creation, so that a pattern in the universe caused a similar pattern to appear among men. Thus the appearance of the sky at the moment of a birth indicated a pattern which harmonized with it in the child born. Newton's theory of gravity seemed to give a scientific basis to this idea of harmonies. In the nineteenth century there was an astrological school of thought that believed that each planet had its own vibrational frequency which, radiating through the ether and mingling with vibrations from other planets, imprinted the soft 'wax' of the new-born child; and another that believed that our natal characters are moulded by X-rays, electromagnetism, 'odic rays' more psychic than physical, and similar forces. However, serious modern astrologers lay more evidence on indications and trends of character and are more interested in linking the impulses in the subconscious minds of their clients with what the stars indicate than they are in forecasting the future. The existing pattern of angular relationships between the sun, moon, planets and birthplace at the moment the umbilical cord is cut synchronizes with the total psychological pattern of potentialities in the new individual. Astrology enables him to know himself.

The work of Jung

A philosophical basis for this belief is sometimes drawn from the writings of the psychologist, C. G. Jung. He is said to have believed that astrology was unreliable; but against this view supporters of astrology quote a letter written by him in 1948 to the editor of the *Indian Astrological Magazine*:

'. . . I've been interested in this particular activity of the human mind since more than thirty years. As I am a psychologist, I'm chiefly interested in the particular light the horoscope sheds on certain complications in the character. In cases of difficult psychological diagnosis I usually get a horoscope in order to have a further point of view from an entirely different angle. I must say that I very often found that the astrological data elucidated certain points which I otherwise would have been unable to understand.'

Jung recognized that astrologers sometimes made startlingly true predictions. He attributed these to factors independent of astrology, especially telepathy, or clairvoyance, using the horoscope as a fulcrum by which to lever up glimpses of the future. Such views might not have been welcomed by astrologers, but they approved of his theory of synchronicity, which stated that everything done at a certain moment of time had the qualities of that moment. Jung chose astrology to test

A mandala drawn by C. G. Jung in 1928. The mandala form is fundamental to many of the great Eastern religions

his theory of synchronicity, a law that was neither chance nor causal. It consisted of two factors: (a) an unconscious image comes into consciousness either directly (that is, literally, as itself), or indirectly (symbolized or suggested) in the form of a dream, idea or premonition; and (b) an objective situation coincides with this context. The one is as puzzling as the other. Jung supported his theory by, among other arguments, analyzing the horoscopes of four hundred married couples. The frequency of the marriage conjunctions of the couples in these charts was not high enough to indicate anything more than chance, but the conjunction of one partner's sun with the other's moon, or the conjunction of two moons came first in order of frequency of all other aspects noted. A higher than chance incidence would have indicated a causal principle, which some people claim astrology supplies and by reason of which it appeals to the modern mind. Instead, there was a meaningful coincidence. One wonders, however, if 400 couples made a large enough sample to justify Jung's conclusion.

But since the qualities of all past moments influence the future, astrological 'progressions' – projections into the future of the potentialities of an individual life – can be argued as justifiable. Weaknesses, strengths, times of prosperity and danger are indicated, but the individual, forewarned, can be fore-armed and choose rightly. Fate is not predestined, although a man's choice may be limited by the character-potentialities within himself and revealed by his chart. Thus, in Marilyn Monroe's case, a time of great danger was indicated by her stars in 1962, especially in July and August (she died on 4 August). Among other relationships of the heavenly bodies astrologically interpreted, that of the sun and Pluto showed a violent end to a period of experience in the twelfth house, which includes self-destruction among its other qualities; and that of Mercury and the sun stimulated intense emotional disturbance under stress.

Modern astrologers agree with Jung that there is no causal link between the planets and events on earth. They indicate trends, periods of possible, perhaps probable, danger or prosperity, but the free will of the native can combat the one or use the other. Though some astrologers, claiming their own creed to be wholly beneficent and sufficient, have attacked

106

Man and the universe: one great energy system?

religion, others affirm that they are religious men who acknowledge a pattern created by God Himself, and that the spiritual factor within each one of us which is the source of our free will can be interpreted through astrology.

Man in the universe

None of the advances of modern knowledge, whether in exact sciences like astronomy or those not subject to exact measurement, such as psychology, have dismayed either astrologers or their myriads of followers, among whom may be numbered many whose intelligence is recognized in their own fields. The fact that a man may be immensely knowledgeable, even a genius, in his chosen activity does not mean that his authority runs in other spheres more than any other man's. There have been been and exist today examples of eminent men who belong to lunatic fringe religious sects and philosophies. But some scientific facts assist the astrologers. They can argue, for example, that the whole of existence is one great energy system. The unit of life, the cell, has a heart to it; cells make up the man, who also has a heart to his centre; the sun is the heart of the solar system which is itself a kind of cell in the Milky Way galaxy, which is again a unit in a pattern of galaxies, and so on.

If it be doubted that man can be physically and mentally affected by the heavenly bodies which inhabit space, it has been pointed out by Aimé Michel, in his preface to Michel Gauquelin's *Astrology and Science*, (1972) (not by an astrologer) that a man is proportionately closer to the stars than he is to the smallest particle known to science within his own body. A man 1.75 metres tall has voluntary control of particles (at least in groups, if not individually) within himself 1,750,000,000,000,000 times smaller than he is. If the electrons in a human body were to become as large as the body, the man himself would stretch to 200 thousand million miles (Pluto, the most distant planet, moves on an axis 4,000 million miles from the sun). To such a gargantuan creature the entire solar system would appear as a tiny whirlpool three and a half centimetres in extent. Since this enormous universe which is myself can affect and be affected by the minute particles of which it is composed, there is nothing *a priori* impossible about the particles called humans being affected by the heavenly bodies; because I am about a thousand times closer to Pluto in space than one of my electrons is to me in size.

Arguments for and against

It is unreasonable to attack astrology as untrue because the theories behind it have changed during the centuries. Few branches of knowledge would escape condemnation if this were the criterion by which their truth was judged. There are more powerful arguments which its critics bring against the astral science, or superstition, as they would call it.

One is the discovery of three new planets, Uranus in 1781, Neptune in 1846 and Pluto in 1930, which upsets the astrologers' mystic seven and, according to their opponents, makes nonsense of all horoscopes before the last date. The astrologers reply that these three planets are so far away and move so relatively slowly that they influence generations

Famous astronomers. From top: John Couch Adams (1819–1892),
Percival Lowell (1855–1916) and Sir William Herschel (1738–1822)

rather than individuals. Even if they had an effect on horoscopes before their discovery, this was so slight as to make little difference to their substantial accuracy (yet Neptune, for example, has been seen to play an important part in Marilyn Monroe's horoscope and must have done in many charts in the past). Some astrologers go further and say that the three new planets had no effect upon human affairs before their discovery, and that their advent brought in new ages of revolution, world movements and scientific advance for mankind. The fact that they were discovered when they were and the implications of their discovery are all part of the grand scheme of things that is patterned in the stars.

Critics say that the planetary aspects as drawn by astrologers are flat patterns on paper. They may establish the celestial latitude and longitude of these bodies, but make no allowances for distance and the velocity of light which, even in heavenly bodies so relatively close, places them not where they appear to be but where they were at the time the light reflected from them started on its journey to us. The apparent positions of the outer planets may therefore be some degrees different from their actual places, and this could fundamentally alter the reading of some horoscopes, slowly though these planets move. To this, the astrologer replies that his art does not exist because the planets cause events to happen but because they symbolically express truth about human beings. Yet the objection remains; why should this symbolism be expressed by two dimensions and not the third?

The precession of the equinoxes

Opponents of astrology make much of the precession of the equinoxes, discovered as early as the second century BC by the Greek astronomer, Hipparchus. This is caused by a very slow change in the earth's axis of rotation which causes the celestial poles to describe circles among the stars, each circle taking 25,800 years to complete. Since the tropical zodiac is out of step with the sidereal zodiac, four thousand years ago the sun at the spring equinox was in the constellation of Aries. From AD 300 until now it has been in that of Pisces, and from about AD 2000 it will be in the constellation of Aquarius (hence the talk nowadays about the dawning of the Age of Aquarius which is

Famous Aquarians. From top: Galileo, Abraham Lincoln, Jules Verne and Mozart

prophesied to be one of universal peace and prosperity). The movement of the celestial poles and equator takes with it the belt of the zodiac with the names of its signs. This means that Taurus now covers the constellation of Aries, and a child born under what was Taurus is given Aries characteristics. Therefore either astrological tradition becomes obsolete as soon as the alignment of signs and constellations ceases or else the qualities attributed to the signs are not connected with the stars at all. Astrologers reply that they use the signs and not the constellations when they state planetary positions, but to an impartial judge this does not seem a very convincing answer.

Practitioners make much of the exact time of birth, and before the view, comparatively modern, that the moment was at the cutting of the umbilical cord, the derisive question was asked as to what happened in a long birth, when the head emerged under one zodiacal sign and the feet under another. The diviners had their answer pat – this indicated a strong head and weak feet (or vice versa!). Another line of attack was that horoscopes should be drawn for the moment of conception, for this was the real time that the new individual began its life, and this was all but impossible to calculate. What is more, the child's organism is wholly formed in the womb, and the metaphor of its being wax upon which planetary influences made their imprint at birth is therefore false. But no less an authority than the great Ptolemy answered the argument in the second century BC by affirming that the stars were in the same relative positions at a birth as at a conception, a hypothesis as impossible to prove as the moment of conception was to pinpoint; and Ptolemy further stated that the birth-moment was of greater importance because a whole human being then began its life, not the mere seed of an embryo.

Astrologers do not agree on house systems and may differ widely on the interpretation of a chart. Neither do doctors agree on treatments nor theologians on the interpretation of the Bible, yet patients continue to trust the former and religious men to be guided by the latter.

If the stars affect men, say astrology's opponents, they must affect all living creatures. Nothing daunted, astrologers have drawn up horoscopes for pets, even for parrots. To some this will appear logical, to others an absurdity.

Astrologers casting a horoscope for the child being born to the woman in the foreground. From Jacob Rueff *De Conceptu et Generatione Hominus*, 1587

'I have never seen a chart that didn't work, if the correct birth time was known,' writes one astrologer. Critics state equally bluntly that life-histories calculated by the stars and real ones do not coincide. They maintain that personal prejudice and mal-observation give a false basis for such a belief. Men remember forecasts that are strikingly correct and forget the hundreds that are wrong; or argue that the successful forecasters have a genuine gift and others err through faulty methods (ignoring the many incorrect predictions allegedly made by even the sometimes successful astrologers).

Astrology and statistics

Individual practitioners are 'wonderful men who are always right', just as individual doctors and treatments, whether genuine or quack, become the fashion, catching the imagination of idle people who have nothing better to do than to make a hobby of hypochondria. But it is claimed that the laws of astrology do not stand up to statistical examination nor can they be shown to be based on scientifically verifiable rules. Those practitioners who have tried to justify astrology by employing statistical methods have, it has been alleged, used it

Michel Gauquelin

incorrectly, and are all the worse for appearing to be learned when they are not.

But statistics, astrologers reply, are irrelevant because, by their very nature, they remove the vital personal element in interpretation. It would be possible to compile an accurate horoscope by feeding all essential data into a computer, but the result would be the difference between Chopin played on a pianola and by a concert pianist. 'The notes are the same but it's not hard to tell the difference.' (Lloyd Cope, *Your Stars are Numbered*, 1971) Since every chart is individual, because no birth can take place at exactly the same place at the same time (one might suggest a conclusive experiment with bunk beds), statistics can deal with only certain features in a birth chart whereas everything is interdependent, and the same factors in a different context could give a different meaning. Statisticians answer that astrologers cannot have it both ways. If they claim that astrology obeys precise laws, such precision can be subjected to statistical analysis, within the recognized limitations of the series of statistics.

But the human spirit defies statistics in individual cases. Even if so precise a statistic could be established as that 100% of bald brown-eyed men, six feet tall, living in Hitchin and buying their suits at Smith's, their shoes at Brown's and their socks at Jones', marry blue-eyed women with wavy blond hair, of five feet, eight inches, coming from Ware, who shop at Tomasina's, Ricarda's and Henrietta's respectively for their tailor-mades, lingerie and handbags, there is no guarantee that the 101st such man will not marry a four foot mulatto from Shepherds Bush. Quite apart from every factor in the chart being given its due weight, some psychic principle seems to be involved in interpretation. The intuition of the astrologer, even the empathy between him and his client, may need to be estimated, and this is beyond statistics. For just as A can have understanding of and affection for B and not C, who nevertheless receives them from D, so one astrologer may have a sympathetic understanding of one client through his chart and another for another. Traditional astrology, it is maintained, can be proved to be effective in such cases, but practitioner and subject must approach it in the right frame of mind and with the right kind of receptivity on both sides.

Attempts to assess accuracy

In *Astrology and Science* Gauquelin quotes various experiments, the verdict of which, he claims, goes against astrology. In the first, fourteen astrologers, picked at random, were given the coordinates of birth of three celebrities and their names and challenged to fit the dates to the names; the results could not have been worse had they answered at random. Practitioners given twenty dates of birth of ten murderers and 'ten dull lives' and asked to separate one group from the other, gave results entirely according to chance. Against this, in *Teach Yourself Astrology* (1970) Jeff Mayo claims that he was one of twenty astrologers who were asked to match ten birth-charts with ten case-histories describing occupations. A control group of twenty who knew no astrology was asked to do the same with the same group of charts and histories. Sixteen of the twenty astrologers predicted better than chance (how much better is not stated) against nine of the control group. The fallibility of statistics of this undetailed kind is shown by the fact that if the sixteen astrologers had scored six out of ten (better than chance) and four had scored five (chance) their total would have been 116; while if the nine non-astrologers had scored seven and the eleven had scored five, their total would have been 118. It is not true to say that one can 'prove anything by statistics', but their exact details must be known if their evidence is to be valid.

Other supporters of astrology contend that blind character analyses from horoscopes can be amazingly accurate in some cases – but what is the proportion of accurate to inaccurate? A psychiatrist who put an astrological advertisement in the paper and sent the same letter to all who replied to it received more than two hundred answers to his letter telling him that he had told the absolute truth. In *Astrology and Science*, Gauquelin himself describes a similar experiment in which he sent out a complete horoscope drawn up by chance and without reference to the sky at birth. He received similar comments. He does not say how many.

To all this astrologers can reply, 'We cannot be blamed for the reactions of gullible men any more than the existence of God is to be questioned on the grounds that there are hundreds of ridiculous sects with ridiculous beliefs who worship Him in

An astrological 'anatomy' showing the signs of the zodiac
superimposed on those parts of the body they affect and govern. The
signs also surround the figure. In the upper corners are two shields of
the French Royal Arms

ridiculous ways. As far as the experiments are concerned, they prove nothing, for there was no personal contact and nothing upon which the personal intuition could seize; and from what is said, we cannot be certain that every necessary factor was included. What does Monsieur Gauquelin mean by "coordinates of birth"? If these did not include everything, if only the date of birth was given and not the moment, then no wonder his experiments failed.'

Faith in astrological powers

In all research into occult phenomena there are always two great impediments. One is that the subjects being investigated may claim to be able to work only under certain conditions; a psychic medium, for example, may claim to be able to move solid objects by telekinetic force only in total darkness. If a researcher demand that he work in light to obviate trickery, he may say that he genuinely cannot. So the researcher goes his way unsatisfied and suspicious, and the medium, however honest, remains suspected and his phenomena discounted.

The other impediment is that faith does seem to make a difference and scepticism or even objectivity does appear to inhibit. There is statistical evidence that experiments in card-guessing and dice-throwing have better results when conducted by groups who believe in extra-sensory perception and precognition than by sceptics. Moreover, there may be genuine grounds for the complaints that some sensitives make when they say, 'I cannot work under these circumstances – the atmosphere is too clinical', or, 'Scepticism inhibits my powers'. It may be that only the faith of the subject can release in the psychologically intuitive astrologer the ability to interpret all the factors in the chart. After all, it should be obvious from the very generalized, even vague, qualities ascribed to the planets, signs and houses, and the fact that virtues and vices are attributed to the same features in different conditions, that there are infinite permutations, combinations and shades of meaning. However strict the rules of interpretation, these need an intuition which is more than rule-of-thumb to understand them. Even when every factor is known and evaluated, interpretation is still pregnant with pitfalls and possible error.

Influence of the heavens on earth

It cannot be denied that the heavenly bodies influence life on earth although the scientists who study them avoid any taint of the astrological spirit in maintaining that the cosmos is indifferent to humankind and takes no interest in the destinies of men. The effect of the moon on the tides has been known for centuries; what has been discovered in our own is the influence it has on certain forms of marine life whose reproductive processes are directly linked to its cycle.

The whole universe is subject to rhythms, and one which particularly affects the earth, although much more evidence is needed for all the results listed below to be certainly attributed to it, is the eleven-year cycle of sun-spots. These appear to govern rainfall and, consequently, water-levels and vegetation, as geological deposits of sediment show. They can shorten days by only a fraction of a second, but enough to cause earthquakes and volcanic eruptions. They cause proliferation of microbes and, perhaps as a result, epidemics. They produce plagues of pests such as locusts; and may be responsible for certain deficiencies in our bodies and even in our minds. As sunspots move towards the peak of their activity there are, it is alleged, significant increases in the incidence of ill-health and sudden deaths. Road accidents, suicides and criminal acts are seemingly affected by solar activity. Diseases of the heart and lungs are associated with solar magnetic disturbances and variations in the sun's cycle apparently affect all life on earth.

The sun's atmosphere stretches so far that our world is actually within it, and where its magnetic atmosphere meets the earth's, disturbances occur which may affect life. Moon and sun, however, are not the only heavenly bodies to affect us. Cosmic rays (discovered in 1926) coming from somewhere in space may influence life on earth. Radio waves coming from the sun and stars were discovered in 1942, and radio interference seems to be influenced by the positions of the moon and planets, while living matter may also be affected by these waves. There is some slightly significant statistical evidence that some solar emanations are related to certain mental illnesses, suggested that magnetic disturbances can affect our brains through interference with their electrical processes. Cosmic forces coming even from the outer space of our own

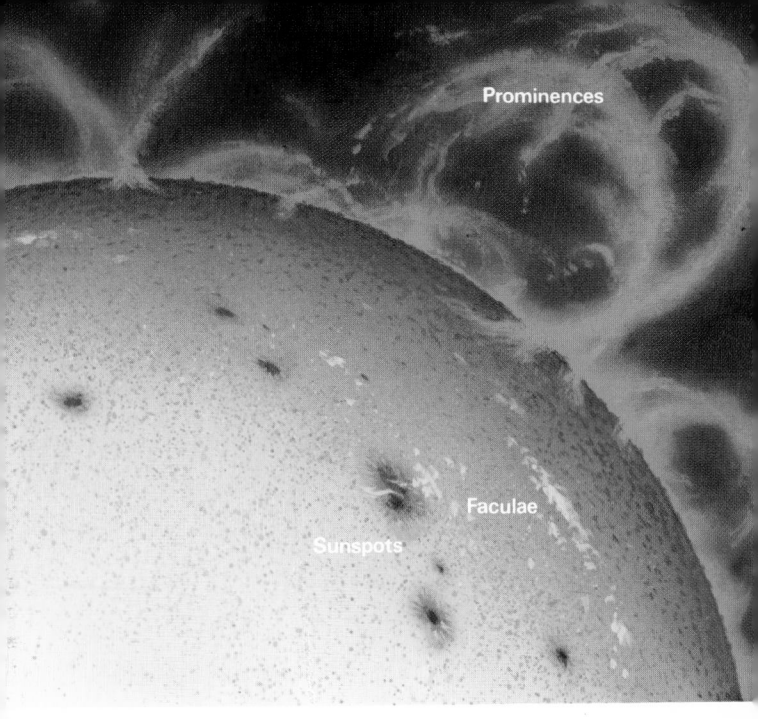

Solar influences on the earth

galaxy may influence chemical reactions, the behaviour of colloids and, more important for us, the nature of water which is found everywhere and forms 60% of our bodies.

The work of Michel Gauquelin

Gauquelin, who summarizes the evidence for the many astonishing physical effects on earth brought about by solar, lunar, planetary and galactic forces, examines astrology and, after weighing it in his balances, finds it wanting. But in doing so, he discovered certain astonishing facts which, in the very destruction of the ancient science, in a sense created it anew. The birth data of 1,084 prominent medical academicians showed that they were born when Mars or Saturn had just risen or were at their culmination. 'Ordinary people never (*sic*) showed this effect and that made matters more surprising.'

Gauquelin followed this study by another on 25,000 celebrities in Germany, Italy, Belgium, Holland and France and discovered that although his subjects were separated by frontiers, customs and languages, a man's profession was indicated by the positions of certain planets at his hour of birth, the most significant results regularly appearing for each planet just after its rise or culmination.

Disallowing any occult explanation, Gauquelin looked for a physical cause. Our genetic code, he argues, has stamped on it our youth, age and maturity — perhaps we can decipher the future as we have learned to do this code. In addition, just as the universe is subject to rhythms acting as cosmic 'clocks', so man has his rhythms and his internal 'clocks', one of which, set at his birth, predetermines particularly illnesses and accidents. Could it be that, rather than that the planets influence the child at his birth, his inner 'clocks' predispose him to enter the world under certain cosmic conditions which correspond to his biological constitution?

If one of a child's hereditary factors is to be born 'under' a particular star, then one of his ancestors must have been born under it too. To discover whether planetary heredity were a general law, Gauquelin matched 15,000 parents and children involving almost 300,000 positions of planets, and discovered a correlation between the birth sky of the parents and that of their children of which the probabilities against chance were 499,999 to one. The indications were clear for Mars, Jupiter, Saturn, the moon and Venus; there was not enough evidence for Mercury, which is very small, nor for Uranus, Neptune and Pluto, which are very distant. What is more, the effects of herditary characteristics were more marked in a child whose birth sky corresponded with that of his parents. The results were consistent with natural births but disappeared when the births were induced, which is to be expected; for if a child, due by nature to be born on 12 April, is induced on 2 April, he will obviously be born under a different sky, and this should be evidence for Monsieur Gauquelin's theory. He could perhaps deduce from the data what day the child would have been born if left to himself.

If Gauquelin's theory proves to be correct, other questions interesting to both astrologers (who may well accept his data without subscribing to his hypothesis) and scientists arise. Do induced births result in different professions being followed? Does the doctor who should have been born under Mars become the actor or playwright if he is 'induced' under Jupiter (presumably specializing in doctor's parts or writing *Doctor in the House*!)? And what of people of poor education or small opportunity who could, according to their stars, have become great doctors – or does Gauquelin mean literally what is quoted from him above that 'ordinary people *never* showed this effect' (my italics)? If so, under what stars are 'ordinary' people born? It is perhaps statistically not enough to show that a high proportion of famous men of a certain type was born under this or that planet; one has to compare them with the great mass of ordinary folk born under the same planet whom fate and circumstances denied the chance of anything but a typist's desk or a shop counter. Rhondda Valley miners in the 1920s (unemployed at that) were not there because all their birth-clocks put them there, nor were they all born under the same stars.

Whatever the answers to such questions may be, Gauquelin denies the existence of any 'planet of the professions' or 'planets of character', suggesting only the presence of cosmic clocks operating in a way as yet unknown but seemingly connected with the rotation of the earth. He also states that there are more conceptions in August and September and that the strongest children are born in May and June – which may indicate only that the first two months are holiday months for Europeans, when mothers who conceive are at their physical best and mentally relaxed.

Whatever the facts, it is certain that traditional astrology, so alive today after seemingly being killed by science, will survive unless and until increased knowledge makes its demise certain and – such is man's reluctance to let go superstition – probably long after that. Until that time, whether or not one believes depends, perhaps, on the stars under which one was born.

GLOSSARY

Ascendant The point of the ecliptic or the sign of the zodiac rising above the horizon at the time of a birth, marriage, etc.

Aspect The relative position of planets as determining their influence at a given time.

Benefic Having a good influence.

Cardinal Having the quality of initiative.

Cusp The first part of a house, especially in nativity calculations; also the dividing line between two houses.

Declination The angular distance of a heavenly body north or south of the celestial equator measured on the great circle passing through the celestial pole and the body; celestial latitude.

Ecliptic The great circle formed by the intersection of the plane of the earth's orbit with the celestical sphere; the apparent annual path of the sun in the heavens.

Elements Fire, air, earth and water.

Ephemeris (pl. **Ephemerides**) Table or tables showing the positions of planets and signs of the zodiac at the time of a birth, marriage, etc, and the prediction of future tendencies, advice of future behaviour etc, based on such a chart.

House One of the twelve divisions of the heavens or celestial sphere having to do with particular aspects of human life – childhood, possessions, etc.

Imum Coeli (I.C.) The lowest point on a chart, at '6 o'clock', opposite the medium coeli (*see below*).

Malefic Having a malign effect.

Medium coeli (M.C.) Mid-heaven, '12 o'clock' on a horoscope.

Mutable Having the qualities of changeableness and adaptability.

Native Astrologically, the subject of a horoscope.

Node (adj. **Nodical**) Either of the two points at which the orbit of a heavenly body intersects a given plane, especially the plane of the ecliptic or of the celestial equator.

Orb The orbit of a heavenly body.

Quadruplicity A set of the four signs of the zodiac which are either cardinal or fixed or mutable.

Retrograde (a) Moving in an orbit in the direction opposite to that of the earth in its revolution round the sun; (b) appearing to move on the celestial sphere in the direction opposite to the natural order of the signs of the zodiac, or from east to west.

Sidereal Time Time determined by the apparent diurnal movement of the stars. (A sidereal day is about four minutes shorter than a solar day.)

Triplicity A set of three signs of the zodiac which belong to the same element.

Zodiac (a) An imaginary belt of the heavens centred on the ecliptic, including all apparent positions of the sun, moon and principle planets, and divided into twelve equal parts, each with its sign; (b) a diagram representing this belt.

BOOKS TO READ

The following list includes only a few of the immense number of books that exist on astrology. It is by no means intended to be exhaustive, but it will serve to start on his road the student who intends to make a serious study of the subject.

An ABC of the Old Science of Astrology by Sidney Randall. Foulsham and Co., London, 1917.

Astrology by Christopher McIntosh. Macdonald Unit 75, London, 1970.

Astrology and Science by Michel Gauquelin. Mayflower Books, London, 1972.

The Astrologers and Their Creed by Christopher McIntosh. Hutchinson, London, 1969.

Astrology, an Historical Examination by P.I.H. Naylor. Robert Maxwell, London, 1967.

The Astrologer's Astronomical Handbook by Jeff Mayo. Fowler, London, 1965.

Astrology for Sceptics by Charlotte Macleod. Turnstone Books, London, 1973.

The Astrology of Personality (2nd edition) by Dane Rudhyar. Servire, The Hague, 1963.

The Case for Astrology by J. A. West and J. G. Toonder. Macdonald, London, 1973.

A Dictionary of Astrology by Dal Lee. Sphere Books, London, 1969.

Elements of Esoteric Astrology by A. E. Thierens. Rider and Co., London, 1931.

An Encyclopedia of Astrology by Sandra Shulman. Hamlyn, London, 1976.

Sun Signs by Linda Goodman. Harrap, London, 1970.

Teach Yourself Astrology by Jeff Mayo. English Universities Press Ltd, London, 1970.

Your Stars are Numbered by Lloyd Cope. Doubleday, New York, 1971.

INDEX

126